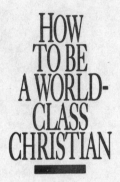

HOW
TO BE
A WORLD-
CLASS
CHRISTIAN

HOW TO BE A WORLD CLASS CHRISTIAN

Paul Borthwick

Paul Borthwick

While this book is intended for the reader's personal enjoyment and profit, it is also designed for group study. A leader's guide with Reproductive Response Sheets is located at the back of this book.

LITERATURE
P.O Box 1047
Waynesboro, GA 30830
ph (706) 554-5827

ISBN: 1884543-22-7

Cover Design: Paul Lewis

Printed in Colombia
Impresso en Colombia

Contents

Foreword

If you've ever felt overwhelmed by the challenges of our world, both near and far, Paul Borthwick has some good news for you. He's reduced the enormous and complex needs of people next door or across the world into manageable chunks so that an individual, small group, Christian education class, or an entire church can get excited about personal involvement.

Paul knows the questions that caring Christians are asking about creative involvement with people outside the walls of the church. His answers are refreshing and he has learned how to tailor suggestions to the gifts, interests, time, and commitment level of members of the body of Christ.

To the person who aspires to be a world-class Christian but says, "I don't know how to get started," he offers several practical "low risk starters." For people with considerable ministry experience he challenges them with a wide variety of "higher and wider risks" in "going global."

His challenge to meet the local needs of people as well as the challenges half a world away is remarkably balanced. He refuses to create any artificial dichotomies between global ministry and outreach right in the community.

He is not triumphal about American wealth or success in the cause of worldwide kingdom ministry, "knowing the Sovereign Judge squelches our feelings of superiority toward any other people on earth." Yet he does not downplay the strategic partnership of American Christians through dozens of creative, practical ministry suggestions.

Finally, he reminds us of the unseen resources at our disposal and the unseen God whom we must trust for anything worthwhile to be accomplished. "Jesus did not command His disciples to run around in frenzied activity trying to meet all the needs. He commanded them to pray that the Lord of the harvest would act."

Paul quotes Tourneir who said, "Life is an adventure directed by God." Here is a wide spectrum of exciting God-given ministry handles for those who refuse to experience the adventures of life vicariously.

Robert A. Seiple
President, World Vision

Acknowledgments

I thank God for the world-class Christians He has surrounded me with at Grace Chapel over the years. They have been the catalysts for my personal growth as well as the sources of many of the ideas found in these pages.

The special catalysts who have stirred me up to grow include the Anzivinos, Longs, Franzonis, Witschis, Dan Dustin, and a host of others on our International Missions Committee and in the Potential Missionary Fellowship.

From a local church leader's perspective, I am thankful for a missions-supportive pastor, Howard Clark. Without the backing of our senior pastor, our attempts to build a world-class vision would be impossible to implement.

My coworkers in the task of missions education, especially Mary Ann Mitchener, Phil Geiger, and Jan Babich, deserve special mention because of their partnership and contribution in a writing project like this.

And most significant of all there is Christie. Without her dedication to the endeavor of world evangelization, my growth would have been stunted. Instead, she has set the pace for simpler living, stimulated my learning about global issues, and endured everything from bedbugs to dysentery to bathroom faucets that spit insect larvae in our travels.

I dedicate this book to her.

Chapter One

WHY BE A WORLD-CLASS CHRISTIAN?

*Once you decide to ask Jesus Christ to take control
of your life, involvement in world missions
is no longer optional.*

Peter Wagner

These are exciting times to be alive. Historians' veins pump with adrenaline when they observe the changes, events, developments, and growth in our world. As Marshall McLuhan predicted, our world has become a "global village." Jet travel, international networks, and interdependent economies have simultaneously shrunk the world while vastly enlarging the amount of information that we try to manage.

In the midst of this expanding base of information and the shrinking global picture, we find ourselves striving to live on a "world-class" scale. Multi-national corporations attempt competition in a global market by reaching the elite distinction of becoming "world-class." Airline advertisements describe Air Canada as "World-Class, Worldwide." Television and sports networks introduce us to "world-class" athletes, and concerts highlight the performances of "world-class" musicians. The adjective "world-class" now describes automobiles, tastes of food, computer technology, hotels, lifestyles, and even disasters.

Dr. Howard Foltz, president of the Association of International Missions Services, writes, "What does it take to be world-class? Florence 'Flo-Jo' Joyner, the tough and flashy runner who won several medals at the 1988 Seoul Olympics, is a world-class athlete who breaks world records. World-class autos are those which forge a sales niche in the world market, so how would you describe a world-class Christian?"[1]

If the business, sports, and media worlds strive to compete on a "world-class" scale, what about the followers of Jesus Christ?[2] Should we too be aiming at world-class excellence in our obedience? Are we to try to relate to the contemporary world so that the Christian faith addresses world-class problems?

The obvious answer is YES! God has given us the privilege of living at one of the most exciting, unique junctures in human history. Through a worldwide community, modern technology, and unparalleled global resources, we in the church of Jesus Christ have the opportunity to interact on a "world-class" scale as never before.

God invites us to His world-class action. How will we respond?

But How?

We respond with a resounding, "Yes, Lord, I want to get on board!" That is, until we start to get a picture of the magnitude . . .

. . . over 5 billion people on earth;

. . . perhaps half of these having never heard of the love of God through Jesus;

. . . millions of starving, homeless, hopeless kids;

. . . urban sprawls of tens of millions of people.

We do not need to carry the descriptions too far. We all experience it—the phenomenon known as "compassion fatigue" the feeling of frustration which laments, "What possible difference could I make?"

The challenge of world-class living overwhelms us — until we begin to reduce the task to manageable chunks. One person likened getting a world vision to eating a 500-pound marshmallow — we know what needs to be done; we simply have no confidence that we can do it nor any idea of where to begin.

This book is about beginnings — simple steps that all of us can take to find our part in God's global action. But first, a few observations about motivation. What will keep us going as we tackle this immense task?

But Why?

With the myriad of challenges that we face in our own personal lives, we need to choose wisely how to invest our time. Is this global pursuit worthwhile? Even if we decide to start toward the world-class growth goal, what motivates us to endure?

Only a few of us will admit it, but we may be quietly asking, "What's in this for me? If I aspire toward 'world-classness,' how will I grow? Will the reward justify the effort?"

Without indulging our self-centeredness to excess, we find motivation as we observe the tangible results in the lives of those growing to be world-class Christians. Let's consider seven areas:

Stimulation. The media and entertainment world has convinced our generation that life is a spectator sport. Like Chauncy the gardener in Peter Seller's film *Being There,* "we like to watch." We watch. We watch while superior athletes compete. We experience adventure vicariously through Indiana Jones, Rambo, or Chuck Norris. Even our faith can become an experience in watching — as pastors, preachers, or dynamic personalities talk or sing or preach to us. Some have become "pew potatoes" — watching rather than participating.

Getting involved in the global scene stirs us to action. As a graduate student, I had the privilege of traveling to Haiti on an "Exposure Trip" designed to show us several international ministries there. When contemplating the trip, I confronted my first obstacle: finances — yet God miraculously made it possible for me to go. Another barrier — I had never flown before, and I (who as a child vomited when being rocked) feared my motion sickness. God took care of me — even on the twelve-seater flight to southwest Haiti, where we had to "buzz" the grass runway to clear off the grazing cows.

Every day for seven days — whether meeting Haitian Christians or speaking through a translator for the first time; whether eating unusual food or confronting a tarantula in the bathroom — I learned afresh what it meant to trust God, especially in the face of my own powerlessness. The involvement in Haiti invigorated my faith.

Very few people have ever come to me for counsel on how to quiet down their personal faith; actually, I can never remember such a request. Most of us look for ways to enliven our faith, not deaden it.

Growing as a globally aware Christian stimulates our faith to develop, as aerating soil stimulates growth in plants. It stirs us up. The pursuit of becoming world-class launches us into a world where we must trust God. Whether it means praying for the funds needed for an international project or walking out to minister in an unfamiliar neighborhood, an outward orientation of our faith encourages us to trust God in direct and practical ways.

One participant on an educational/service project to Egypt wrote: "I think the greatest lesson I learned on this trip was how to deal with difficult situations. . . . I learned this lesson because, with the nature of the trip, one had to learn these lessons to endure the experience. The work was hard, conditions uncomfortable, and amenities barely adequate—but with God's help I could withstand this and grow in my faith through the experience."

Pursuing the world-class goal puts us personally into the action. Rather than experiencing life vicariously through those that we watch, *we move from being spectators to participants*. Reaching out in what might be risky relationships or volunteering for sacrificial service moves us out of our comfort zone into the arena of dependence on Christ. And, like Peter on the water, when we step out in faith, Jesus meets us there!

Focus. Don observed his own ability to be swayed by cultural opinions and current trends. He concluded, "I am the disciple of the last man who spoke."

Don illustrates the tensions we all face regarding priorities, choices, and a clarified focus on our lives. The advertisements dictate to us what we must have to be acceptable—whether cars, clothes, vacations, or perfume. We follow the advice of a pluralistic world that dictates standards of success, but we find ourselves being torn apart. In one way or another, we fall prey to becoming cultural Christians rather than true disciples.

Tom Sine, futurist and consultant, wrote: "We all seem to be trying to live the American Dream with a little Jesus overlay. We talk about the lordship of Christ, but our career comes first. Our house in the 'burbs comes first. Upscaling our lives comes first. Then, with whatever we have left, we try to follow Jesus."[3]

We need help in focusing our lives.

In spite of the magnitude, a global awareness helps us do just that. Alertness to the needs of others, concern for the broken people of our world, and ideas of how to respond practically give us a new sense of priorities. Rather than an unhealthy preoccupation with the question, "Am I fulfilled?" we find ourselves asking how we can help others—and, in so doing, we find the fulfillment we were looking for in the first place.

A businessman in the financial district of Boston told me that serving meals at a soup kitchen for Boston's homeless clarifies the meaning of his life. "It makes me see myself as a fellow-struggler with these people, and this helps me keep my world and my problems in perspective."

Joy. Similar to that businessman, the Lands family added perspective to their lives by serving the Thanksgiving meal at a shelter for the homeless. Rather than gorging themselves on the typical—"I ate too much, where's the Alka-Seltzer?"— Thanksgiving dinner, they decided to go out to serve. Their practical yet sacrificial service produced greater thankfulness than they had known on any previous Thanksgiving.

One of the teenage daughters reflected, "At first we thought we would feel more thankful because we would realize how much more we had than these people did . . . but the greatest memory of the day for me is joy: These folks who seemed to have nothing could give and experience joy together. Sharing in their joyful simplicity taught us far more than we gave them."

Venturing out into our exciting, frightening, hurting world teaches us that Jesus-type joy is joy in the face of hardship, joy in spite of the surroundings. An outward focus puts us in touch with the joy that Paul the Apostle had in jail when he wrote in his most joy-filled epistle, "Rejoice in the Lord always" (Phil. 4:4). And this joy keeps us going through the roller-coaster ride of life.

Relevance. I asked a number of unchurched people their opinions about Christians: "Who would you say is the best example of Christianity the way it's supposed to be?"

A few answered "Billy Graham" because of his public integrity, but the vast majority answered "Mother Teresa of Calcutta." The reason? "Because she's the only one that I see who treats poor people the way that Jesus would."

Nobody commented much about her theology, her nun's habit, or her tiny stature. The dominant feature of Mother Teresa in the minds of these secular people was her active, demonstrated faith. Their comment reminded me of the rebuke attributed to the existentialist Nietzche: "His disciples will have to look more saved if I am to believe in their Saviour."

Growing as a world-class Christian helps us "look more saved." When we explain that we spent our weekend helping people insulate their homes or serving at a nursing home, people may inquire more about the faith that motivates such action. When we spend a vacation visiting missionary friends, people ask us about our experiences, which inevitably leads to a discussion of our beliefs.

World-class involvement builds credibility because we begin to take an interest in world-class issues—whether political, religious, or environmental. My wife, Christie, strives to address the Gospel values to rain-forest destruction in South America; in so doing, she is able to integrate her faith to issues raised by environmental activists. One non-Christian man came to hear me preach because I gained credibility in his eyes by getting involved in the township of Soweto, South Africa.

An outward focus of our faith—integrated into our world and addressed to real needs and issues—establishes our witness to the mercy of Jesus as credible, demonstrable, and relevant. Our world needs to see followers of Christ who indeed love mercy and do justice (Micah 6:8).

In the ever-shrinking global village that God sends us into, the world is asking, "What type of neighbors will these Christians be?" When we dive into service and start participating in the demonstration of Jesus' love, people start paying attention.

Direction. Stephanie started growing as a world-class Christian several years ago. For her, that growth led to involvement with international students, most notably scholars from the People's Republic of China. Working together with several friends, she used her gift of hospitality to entertain, feed, and love dozens of Chinese visitors.

After a few years of this ministry, she decided to go to China for a visit. She took a leave of absence from her engineering firm and traveled five weeks in China, staying with men and women whom she had befriended on their visits to the United States. After a rugged trip, including bronchitis and a stint in a Beijing hospital, I thought Stephanie would be quitting her ministry to the Chinese or at least she would never travel again.

Quite the contrary! After her return, she made contact with the English Language Institute. She applied, was accepted and trained, and is now teaching English at a technical school in Beijing.

Outreach into the world beyond her normal sphere of influence put Stephanie in a new position to hear God. Her firsthand involvement gave new direction to her life. Not everyone gets so radically redirected. Some find new ways to use their skills to serve—like Bob, a Boston architect. He heard of an urban mission that needed help as they redesigned and refurbished their building to house residents. In his spare time, and at no cost to the mission, he used his architectural skills to design a new wing for the mission. In so doing, he saved them thousands of dollars while feeling the satisfaction of using his skills to help others.

Or consider Pat, who uses her teaching skills to tutor urban students once a week. By her time spent with students, she has built a new network of friends, developed a new appreciation for the city, and helped students go from "F's" to "B-'s."

When we get tired of "grabbing for all the gusto" because we find it empty or dissatisfying, God says, "I have a better way: service on behalf of others." Jesus taught it—if you want to be great, become a servant; if you want to be first, then become last (Mark 10:43-45). Jesus' paradox: We gain by losing; we lead by serving; we find ourselves by giving ourselves away. In the process of serving we find new purpose and direction for the skills, abilities, and resources that He has given us.

Sneak Previews. Any major motion picture lures us out early to catch the sneak previews so that (I presume) we can be the first to be able to describe the characters and plot to our friends.

God invites us to a sneak preview too. Through growth as world-class Christians, we have the unique opportunity of getting a sneak preview of heaven, where those from every nation, tribe, people, and language will worship Jesus together (Rev. 7:9).

As a participant of the Lausanne II Conference in Manila, I marveled at the opening and closing ceremonies, where representatives from 190 countries—in national dress, some with flags, others with instruments—led our celebration and our singing. People from many races, tribes, languages, and countries gathered together to sing praise to Jesus, the Lamb of God, who takes away the sins of the world. I thought to myself, "This is what heaven will be like!"

In a microcosm, we can get similar previews by worshiping with believers from other countries, who worship in other languages, follow other traditions, and sing in different tones. Without traveling more than twenty miles, I can worship with brothers and sisters from Brazil, China, Laos, or Haiti. As I worship with them — with all of the cultural "dressing" their service might include — I develop an enlarged vision of the body of Christ. This in turn enlarges my vision for His world and my vision of who He is — the Lord of the universe, the hope of the world.[4]

Pleasure. Put simply, our efforts to grow as world-class Christians pleases God. It pleases God because in the process we imitate Christ (Phil. 2:5-11) — serving without reciprocation. Every year, our church sends out volunteers to serve in various ways on mission teams. At least once each summer someone is asked, "Well, who pays you to do this?"

The team member explains, "No one. Actually, we pay to be able to serve on the team."

The amazed inquirer inevitably responds, "You mean you *pay to work?*"

They pay to serve because they are following the example of Jesus, who paid (with His own life) for the opportunity to serve us — even while we were still spiritually dead in our sins! (Rom. 5:8)

Outward-focused serving pleases God because it puts us at His disposal — workers in His "harvest fields" (Matt. 9:36-38). Developing a world-class discipleship pleases God because in so doing, we break out of the entrapments of cultural Christianity and open ourselves to see Him with greater love and to serve Him with renewed vigor.

You Are Invited — Do You Accept?

I feel hurt when I find out, after the fact, that my friends had a party and I was not invited. Whether by reason of unintentional oversight or deliberate rejection, no one likes to be left out.

The good news is this: God invites us into His worldwide action! No one is left out. The magnificent, awesome task requires every Christian to participate. We cannot do it alone, but we join together so that as we grow to be world-class Christians, the world-class church will get God's work—the Great Commission[5]—done.

David Bryant, leader of a movement called "Concerts of Prayer," teaches that God's primary goal is *not* to get each of us into the Great Commission. His goal is to get the Great Commission *into us!* God invites us into His worldwide action in order to change our lives. As we jump in, it will make us more like Jesus and help us to experience all that God has for us. Let's go for it!

Chapter Two

WHAT IS A WORLD-CLASS CHRISTIAN?

*Anthropologists . . . explain that at our cores is
a basic view of reality—a worldview. That
worldview determines who we are, what we value,
and how we behave.*

Gordon Aeschliman

I had been anticipating the trip to San Francisco for months.
As a native of the Northeast, I had never been to this great
city, although travel brochures, television shows, and other
travelers had enticed me many times. I will admit that part of
my reason for accepting the invitation to speak at the seminar
was the time it would give me to explore San Francisco.

The seminar was about five hours old when the room began to shake. It felt like a gigantic underground train was
passing directly below our room. People clamored for the
door. The earth was moving, and we ran out just in time to
see the elevator shaft of the hotel across the street rip away
from the building and collapse.

It took us all several minutes to realize that we had just
come through the worst earthquake that San Francisco and
the Bay Area had experienced in many years. Within twelve
hours, the seminar was canceled, and we were all scrambling
for any flight that would take us out of town. My "tour" of
San Francisco never occurred.

As I sat on the airplane en route to Boston, I was impressed by all the times I had heard the term world-class in the past thirty-six hours. I recorded them in my journal. I flew on a world-class airline into a world-class city, stayed at a world-class hotel where they claimed to serve world-class cuisine. Then there was the world-class disaster which would receive world-class news coverage all over the earth.

I concluded in my journal, "What does it mean to be world-class?"

Contemporary Definitions

When I started challenging Christians by using the term world-class, the responses were mixed. Some loved it, thinking that I was encouraging an excuse to live a lavish lifestyle, fly on the Concorde, or indulge in rich foods. Others were deeply disturbed because they felt that no Christian should care about the things our culture calls world-class.

There is no consensus on what this recently-created adjective means. For some, it means "able to compete with the finest athletes in the world." This is certainly the meaning when we call Olympic competitors world-class athletes. In business, it usually refers to the ability to compete in a global economy, so a hotel chain or an airline advertises itself as "world-class."

World-class might mean "lofty", as in the phrase in a *Reader's Digest* note which advocated unstructured time which allowed one to think "world-class thoughts." It could simply mean "international"; I read the ingredients of a salad dressing mix which listed "these world-class spices." It may be used to set something apart from the average or mundane, as in the "world-class wardrobe" of some millionairess.

Any of these definitions could carry over with meaning to the follower of Jesus Christ. We should aspire to be relevant on a worldwide scale, able to hold our own in discussions about world events, concerned about a faith that is truly international, and committed to being above the average in all our endeavors. But there is more.

For the Follower of Jesus

A brochure came in the mail the other day inviting our investment in international stocks. On the cover, there was a map of the earth, but all countries had been deleted except the United States, which had been expanded to cover all of the global landmass. The caption read, "Because the World Doesn't Look Like This, Neither Should Your Investment Portfolio." Inside, the advertisers tried to convince us that an international, interdependent world demanded world-class investing in foreign as well as domestic accounts.

The caption stirred my thinking about us as followers of Jesus Christ. Because the world does not look like just the United States, neither should our world vision. Because the world is much larger than United States culture, our prayers should be larger than just our normal sphere of influence. Because God is God of all nations, we dare not imply that He somehow belongs exclusively to ours. He calls us to be world-class Christians.

But what does that mean? Consider this definition of a world-class disciple of Jesus Christ: "A world-class Christian is one whose lifestyle and obedience are compatible, in cooperation, and in accord with what God is doing and wants to do in our world."

Let's evaluate the key words.

Lifestyle and Christian Obedience. We are not talking about some compartment of faith that affects only our concepts and perspectives. If we are trying to obey Jesus, it affects every part of our lifestyle. To borrow the analogy from Robert Boyd Munger's *My Heart, Christ's Home*, it is as if our lives were a house, and each room represented some specific aspect of

our lives. Our kitchen represents our appetites, our bedrooms our sexuality, our recreation rooms our leisure, and
our closets the things we keep hidden from outsiders.

When we come to Jesus, He asks for entrance into every
room. If He is Lord of our lives, we cannot be satisfied to
keep Him in the sterile hospitality of the living room; He
wants free reign of the house.

Peter's encounter with Cornelius, the God-fearing Gentile
of Acts 10, illustrates God's ability to break into our closed
"rooms" so that we might submit totally to His control. In
Peter's worldview, it was totally legitimate to exclude Gentiles from the Gospel. As a member of the chosen people of
Israel, Peter could assume that the Messiah Jesus had come
only for His people. But God broke through, using a repeated
dream. When Peter was obedient, he realized that, "God does
not show favoritism but accepts men from every nation who
fear Him and do what is right" (Acts 10:34-35). When Peter
allowed the Holy Spirit to have free reign, his world vision
was enlarged.

My older friend, Marion, illustrates an obedient lifestyle in
another way. As she approached her retirement, she could
have followed the cultural norm of keeping these years of
rest to herself. She might have thought, "I've worked long
and hard for this; I deserve a few years in the sun." Instead,
she let Jesus into every "room" of her life, including the
room called retirement or entitled rest.

She committed her retirement years to the Lord's service,
including her years of accumulated experience in mass food
production. After two months of retirement, she departed for
a children's orphanage in Haiti where she served for five
months training people in mass food production. Now, five
years and a half-dozen trips to Haiti later, she does even
more. She gets plenty of time in the sun, but she uses that
time running Bless the Children of Haiti ministries, an orga-

nization committed to the support and feeding of 300 children in that economically-troubled country. Through her Christian lifestyle and obedience, Marion has influenced dozens of others to go to Haiti to offer some sort of service. Through their partnership with Haitian pastor Franklin Val, hundreds of children now eat at least one nutritious meal per day.

Be Compatible. As Christie and I wrapped up our day at Walt Disney World, she went to take a few more pictures. I asked if I could rest by sitting on the benches at the end of "Main Street USA." As I rested in this recreated town square of what was supposed to be an image of average American life, I started listening to the conversations going on around me. One exhausted family argued with each other in Spanish. Another spoke German and others conversed in Japanese. I sat there about twenty minutes and heard six different languages being spoken.

The experience reflects real life. On "Main Street USA," the multicultural dynamic of our modern world was being played out. The image stuck in my mind as a picture of the ethnically diverse, internationalized world into which we are called. Even if we live in places that were once shrines to Americana, they are now pictures of the global village. This is where we strive to be compatible with what God wants to do through us.

The dictionary defines compatible as "existing together in harmony." The world-class Christian is one who desires his or her life to be in total harmony with God's purposes for His world. In other words, we want to find ourselves in line with His will.

Jonah illustrates one who at first resisted being "compatible" with God's purposes. He ran in the opposite direction from God, but through some gentle persuasion by God's sovereign intervention, Jonah turned around. He decided (somewhat by force, I suppose) that being in harmony with God's purposes was better than running.

But Jonah is an example for all of us. When I read a futurist's prediction that the world's economy cannot support the current affluent lifestyle of the United States, I would rather run like Jonah than ask hard questions about what needs to be cut out of my own lifestyle to be more in harmony with God's worldwide purposes.

The world-class Christian is willing to wrestle not only with what it means to be compatible with God's purposes but also with what it means to live in harmony with our brothers and sisters in Christ around the world. As we grow to understand what God is doing in the world, we cannot help but be challenged in our lifestyles, our commitment, and our zeal by our fellow believers in the non-Western world.

Cooperation is a key. When Christie and I get in a canoe, we would be good candidates for an entry in "America's Funniest Home Videos." If we do not tip over, we row in circles, or we simply swamp the canoe slowly. Even though we have been told what we are doing wrong, we struggle to work together for effective forward progress.

Canoeing dramatically illustrates the need to work together. If she rows one way and I another, we go in circles. If we do not balance our weight, the canoe tips over. To get the canoe to do what it is supposed to, we need to work cooperatively.

In the same way, to accomplish what God intends for us in His world, we must be working cooperatively with Him and each other. This means basic obedience to the truths revealed in His Word, but it also means a radical willingness to turn away from aspects of our culture which may be acceptable in popular opinion but are "rowing" counter to the purposes of God.

Peter did this when he reached out to the Gentiles, engaging himself in a ministry that his culture called unclean but God declared clean. Jesus cooperated with the purposes of God by reaching out to lost, lonely, rejected sinners. To be a friend of tax collectors and prostitutes was more important to Him than popular opinion, because He was committed first of all to declaring the mercy of God.

Perhaps the most dramatic biblical "cooperator" of all, Ananias, meets us in Acts 9. We know only that he was a "disciple in Damascus." God calls him to go minister to Saul, the terrorizing fanatic of the Pharisees who had recently overseen the stoning of Stephen and was presently on a rampage against the church.

Ananias voices his concerns (Acts 9:13-14), but the Lord says "Go!" Ananias obeys, takes his life in his hands, and enters the house where Saul is staying. Cooperating with God's purposes takes priority even over his own safety. His opening words reveal the depth of his obedience: "Brother Saul" (Acts 9:17). It is like a Jew saying to a Nazi, "Brother." If we have never faced an enemy who has done us physical or emotional harm, we cannot fathom the depth of emotion that must have filled Ananias. He faces a man against whom he had probably prayed only days earlier, and he says, "Brother!" Actions of the past dissipate like smoke, and he opens his arms to welcome Saul into God's family. Ananias knew what it was to keep his own feelings secondary in exchange for cooperating with the higher purposes of God.

Cooperating with God's purposes may not be as drastic as Ananias' experience. A sixth-grade teacher at a Christian school visited East Germany in the summer of 1989. The sight of the Berlin Wall overwhelmed her because of what it represented; so when school began in September, she asked her students to join her every day in prayer for the political freedom of East Germany.

Late in 1989, the Berlin Wall began to be dismantled, and East Germans gained freedom that many of them had never before experienced. The boys and girls of that sixth-grade class exulted that year with an amazing sense of having cooperated in prayer together with the purposes of God.

Living in Accord. I mentioned earlier the results of my informal survey about outstanding Christians. Almost without exception, Mother Teresa stands out in peoples' minds. Why? Because she lives in accord with what God wants to do in the world. She is credible. Her actions speak louder than her words, and her lifestyle preaches the love she professes to believe.

To be credible is to be genuine. James exhorts us toward credibility when he tells us that "faith without works is dead" (James 2:26). He writes, "Suppose a brother or sister is without clothes and daily food. If one of you says to him, 'Go, I wish you well; keep warm and well fed,' but does nothing about his physical needs, what good is it?" (James 2:15-16)

It is far better to document our faith by works than it is to have faith alone (James 2:18); even the devils have a semblance of faith (James 2:19). James exhorts us to credible, demonstrated faith.

The Apostle John reiterates the point. He defines love based on our demonstrated acts of mercy toward those in need: "If anyone has material possessions and sees his brother in need but has no pity on him, how can the love of God be in him? Dear children, let us not love with words or tongue but with actions and in truth" (1 John 3:17-18).

The world-class Christian is committed to growing toward a credible demonstration of faith "with actions and in truth."

Even Jesus demonstrated His credibility by His outward good works. When the disciples of John the Baptist were looking for proof of Jesus' Messiahship, He responded by highlighting His treatment of the broken: "The blind receive sight, the lame walk, those who have leprosy are cured, the deaf hear, the dead are raised, and the Good News is preached to the poor" (Matt. 11:5).

Our world desperately needs Christians who live in accord with God's will and demonstrate credible faith by their lives. Consider Chuck Colson. Perhaps the reason that he has maintained such high respect in our world has little to do with his books or his speaking engagements. Instead, it is his affinity for and commitment to prisoners. An inmate in Latin America said, "Anyone who will come into this stinking prison and share his food with me is worth listening to." Credibility provides the foundation for effective witness.

In Our World. A pocket-size book arrived the other day. The cover promised me that it contained a "compact guide to the Christian life." I scanned the pages, and to my chagrin, there was not one reference in the 226 pages to a Christian's commitment to be world-minded, globally aware, or missions-oriented. Sadly, it reflected the attitudes of many who say, "Well, there are so many needs right here at home that we cannot think beyond our worlds."

In contrast to such a narrow view, Gordon Aeschliman, editor of *World Christian* magazine, defines the world we find as we approach the year 2000:

In a village a thousand miles up the Amazon, people are reading the French-owned magazine *Elle* and the U.S.-produced *Better Homes and Gardens*. Guatemalans are ordering chicken chow mein, American youth are wearing Russian designer jeans, the Japanese are displaying their latest cuts at top Paris fashion shows, the French are eating Big Macs, the world is doing the lambada, and Japanese Ninja Turtles have given Batman the boot.[1]

In such an internationalized world, even a compact guide to the Christian life must include a global perspective. The world-class commitment is to the "ends of the earth" (Acts 1:8), not just the end of the street or the extent of our zip code. God calls us out of our church pews and beyond our own comfort zones into other cultures where we may confront differing worldviews and varying understandings of religion. Like the people of Israel, we follow the Lord of the universe who reminds us that it is "too small a thing" for us to be preoccupied with ourselves; instead, His plan is to make us a "light" for those outside the Gospel so that "you may bring my salvation to the ends of the earth" (Isa. 49:6).

At a nearby seminary, John Stott told the story of visiting a tiny church in rural England while on a study leave. He worshiped with them every Sunday, participated in their fellowship, and heard their discussions. He related his dismay when week after week, the pastor would preach about issues facing the village, pray about concerns in the church, and discuss decisions related only to their congregation. "I came to the conclusion," Stott observed, "that these people worship a *village God.*"

Our God is not some sort of "village God," existing for our concerns alone and isolated to our worlds. He is the Lord of the universe, the God to whom all will give an account, the Saviour who reaches out through His church to all who need to know His love regardless of ethnic background, economic standing, or geographic location.

The world-class perspective remembers to focus on a global God who calls us onto His team.

Lessons From a World-Class Disaster
From a world-class city in a world-class disaster, the question arises, what does it mean to be world-class? For the follower of Jesus, it means abandonment of self to Him and His pur-

poses. It means giving ourselves to His world so that people may see our lives as living illustrations of the Gospel. It means being His people in the world to the point that people will begin to recognize us as having been with Jesus (Acts 4:13) because our lifestyles and actions are marked by His imprint.

In *The Grapes of Wrath*, John Steinbeck summarizes the lives of several people with these tragic words: "When they died, it was as if they had never lived." They made no impact, left no legacy, affected no lives.

In contrast, the teacher in the popular movie, *Dead Poet's Society*, challenged his students with the words, *carpe diem* — "seize the day." He stirred them to make their lives extraordinary: "the powerful play [of life] goes on and you may contribute a verse." The spirit of such words grips us. We all want to make a difference. We all want to offer a contribution to God's worldwide purposes.

We fear Steinbeck's tragic epitaph, but the solution to our fears is found in Jesus. As we give ourselves to be His world-class followers, we can be His agents of change in our broken world. We can be His world-class disciples.

Chapter Three

THE SCRIPTURES AND THE SAINTS

Our God is a missionary God.
John Stott

The tragic story of Hank Gathers filled the sports news for weeks. This young man, a promising center on the basketball team of Loyola Marymount University, died during a game as a result of complications caused by an irregular heartbeat. The grief of the team and the school spread across the country.

A short while after his death, the Loyola Marymount team entered the NCAA tournament. They dedicated their playing time to their fallen comrade, Hank. One player, Hank's best friend, shot his first free throw each game left-handed— Hank's shooting hand. Emotions ran high.

The Loyola Marymount team, playing without their star center, was not expected to go far in the NCAA tournament. But they won the first game, and the emotions intensified. The players openly spoke of winning the tournament for Hank. They won again, dethroning the past year's champion. A third time they defeated a team that possessed superior talent. The sports commentators turned their attention to one repeated question, "How far can this emotion take them?"

The answer came quickly. The team was defeated in the next round by an enormous margin by the team that would eventually win the tournament. Emotion could not sustain them.

The scene could be repeated in many of our lives. In the face of death—more specifically, in the face of the many deaths of people in our world who suffer in hardship, starvation, and ignorance of the Gospel—we fill up with emotion. The image of thousands or millions perishing without Christ can stir our emotions deeply. Such a vision can lead to zeal, commitment to the cause of Christ, and an overwhelming desire to win the spiritual battle.

But the commentators who watch our emotional zeal step back and ask, "How far will this emotion take them?" And—like the Loyola Marymount team—we find out that emotion is not enough. Faced with overwhelming odds and our own feelings of helplessness, emotion cannot sustain us. We need two foundation stones in our vision to sustain our commitment to grow as world-class Christians.

The Biblical Perspective

The first foundation stone we need is the Word of God. Oswald Chambers, writer of the devotional classic *My Utmost for His Highest*, reminds us that "the basis of missionary appeals is the authority of Jesus Christ, not the needs of the heathen."[1] In other words, we commit ourselves to growth as world-class Christians because Jesus says so in His Word, not because it is the popular or emotionally attractive thing to do.

In the mid-1980s, the world's attention turned toward the plight of famine-ravaged people in Ethiopia and the Sudan. An enormously successful concert raised millions of dollars to help alleviate the suffering. At that time, talking about the "Sahel region," discussing the injustices being done toward Eritrean people, and giving sacrificially to assist the hungry gave one admittance into the popular limelight.

Eighteen months after the concert, however, attentions had turned elsewhere. The emotional appeal of northern Africa had dissipated, and projects which had been initiated during the "boom" of giving were abandoned half-completed because the money, like the soil of these countries, had dried up.

Why? Because emotions cannot sustain the mission. They are necessary and operate effectively as catalysts, but they are not enough. Our vision for being involved as world-class Christians must be built on the sure foundation of God's Word. Our global commitment emanates out of the heart of God, not out of some popular fad of our times.

We build our vision and sustained involvement on the purposes of God as revealed in His Word.

Genesis introduces us to the global God, the Creator of the ends of the earth. The first family is commanded to be fruitful and multiply and fill the earth. God's desire is that mankind, His highest creation, would enjoy and fill the whole earth over which He reigns as Lord.

Genesis also teaches us the origins of evil in our world, an independent spirit that led to sin. But once more, God shows Himself to be the divine pursuer, looking for fallen mankind and seeking to restore Adam and Eve to fellowship with Himself.

In Genesis, we also meet the world-class father of faith — Abraham. We learn that God desires to bless all the nations of the earth through him. Abraham, the prototypical missionary, is sent across land and across cultures that he might be a blessing to all people. Abraham's great-grandson, Joseph continues the universal blessing theme as Genesis concludes. Through Joseph, Egypt, the tribes of Israel, and indeed "many lives" (Gen. 50:20) are saved.

The Law teaches God's standards of behavior in a broken

and sin-filled world. The people of Israel are the primary recipients of this Law, but recurrent throughout the laws governing relationships is God's expressed desire to show kindness and mercy toward the poor, the disenfranchised, the weak, and the "outsider."[2]

The Law provides our biblical foundation for reaching out to displaced and defenseless people like the homeless, the alien, the refugee, or the international student. Even in this section of the Scriptures that many of us regard as harsh and even irrelevant to our times, God reveals His heart for the hurting and lonely and broken.

The Books of History open our eyes to God's people in action, marching forward in conquest for His purposes and reaching out in mercy to those outside of the chosen people.

While we abhor the violence and do not always understand God's purposes in the conquests, we nevertheless see His people marching forward. Countless missionary pioneers in new cultures have gained courage from God's promise to Joshua, that "I will give you every place where you set your foot" (Josh. 1:3).

In these books, we learn of Naaman the Syrian, Rahab the harlot, and Ruth, the devoted daughter-in-law of Naomi, all Gentiles but nonetheless illustrations of faith. The books of history teach us of our call into the world, even as we see the victories and failures of those that have gone before us.

The Psalms enlarge our vision of worship as they turn our attention upward to the God of all nations. They exhort us to "declare His glory among the nations" (Ps. 96:3) and remind us that "the heavens declare the glory of God" (Ps. 19:1).

The psalms keep us from fretful anxiety about the plight of our world, commanding us to "Be still, and know that I am God; I will be exalted among the nations, I will be exalted in the earth" (Ps. 46:10). Amy Carmichael, facing the staggering hardships of India from without and personal suffering within, found her reassurance in this verse. Leading her ministry for many years from her sickbed, she had only two pictures in her room: one framed the words, "Be still," and the other, "I know." The psalms gave her calm assurance that the sovereign God would lead her as her shepherd, even through the valley of the shadow of death.

The psalms teach us that we serve as His agents in the earth, but that "all the ends of the earth will fear Him" (Ps. 67:7). These words of worship give us perspective. God is guiding the nations of the earth (Ps. 67:4), ruling forever by His power and watching over all of the peoples of the earth (Ps. 66:7). We cannot go wrong if we are submitted to Him.

The Prophets speak the oracles of God, calling the people of faith back from their sin and directing them to be the light of revelation to the Gentiles and to all nations, bringing His salvation to the ends of the earth (Isa. 49:6). In the prophets, men of faith exhort the people of Israel out of their lives of comfort into outreach and ministry.

Even in the face of captivity and suffering, the prophets keep the vision of global revival in front of the people, with both Isaiah and Habakkuk predicting the day when the earth would be full of the knowledge of the Lord as the waters cover the sea (Isa. 11:9 and Hab. 2:14). These prophets direct us toward the coming Messiah, the one who will come to "proclaim peace to the nations," establishing a rule "from the Euphrates to the ends of the earth" (Zech. 9:10).

In the Gospels the promised Messiah arrives in humility, with His first worshipers representing the breadth of His reign: There are the economic/social outcasts (the shepherds) along with the aged, like Simeon and Anna, but there are also the royal, the foreign kings who came from the East (the first non-Gentile worshipers).

By His coming, Jesus set the precedent for servanthood and love for the lowly:

From golden streets and angel choirs,
To dirt floors and lowing cattle
Jesus emptied Himself
That we might be full.[3]

The Lamb of God arrives at the start of the Gospels, lives out His divine purpose, and purchases salvation for any in the world who believe on Him (John 3:16) through His death and resurrection. Then, after demonstrating His power over death, He commands His followers to take the Good News of salvation to all people, preaching repentance, making disciples, and openly identifying themselves with their Lord.[4]

The Book of Acts illustrates the early church carrying out Jesus' mandate. The promised power of the Holy Spirit comes on them and the witness begins. They declare the Gospel boldly in Jerusalem, starting to obey Acts 1:8, but it takes some persecution to get them out into Judea and Samaria (Acts 8:1).

Gradually, the ethnocentric spirit of Christianity as a Jewish sect is exchanged for the glorious diversity of an Ethiopian, the Samaritans, and even Gentiles entering the family of faith. With the entry of the Gospel to the Gentiles, we meet Paul the Apostle who will commence the spread of the Gospel to the "ends of the earth."

The work of the Spirit in the Christian body drove the people of Christ outward. They simply could not stop speaking about what they had seen and heard (Acts 4:20).

The Epistles, written to churches planted by first-century missionaries, establish the fledgling church in faith and doctrine so that they could in turn be proclaimers of the Gospel to others. In the face of their own hardships, the churches nevertheless turned outward so that their faith was becoming known everywhere (1 Thes. 1:8).

The writers kept the vision of the worldwide Gospel before

their readers. Paul reminded the Romans of his aspiration to proclaim Christ where He had never been preached (Rom. 15:20), and he instructed Timothy concerning God's desire for all to be saved and come to know the truth (1 Tim. 2:4).

Peter developed this same theme (2 Peter 3:9) while encouraging his readers to stand strong in solidarity with their brothers throughout the world (1 Peter 5:9). James calls for genuine religion demonstrated by care for widows and orphans (James 1:27), and John exhorts demonstrated (not just spoken) love (1 John 3:18).

The writers of these epistles wanted their readers (including us!) to be established firmly in the faith that should be proclaimed worldwide. They wrote to affirm our election in Jesus Christ, understanding that this would lead to "the destruction of our prejudices and our parochial notions and our patriotisms; we are turned into servants of God's own purpose. [We come to realize that] the whole human race was created to glorify God and enjoy Him forever."[5]

The Book of Revelation consummates the history started in God's creation in Genesis. In contrast to the city of Cain, established out of rebellion and sin, we are ushered into the city of God, the place where there is no need for light because God Himself is the light.

And in this great throng of worshipers at the throne of the Lamb of God, we have the global God adored by His people that have come to love Jesus Christ. These people have come from every nation, tribe, people, and language (Rev. 7:9). Their linguistic and cultural differences melt away in insignificance as they join together in a chorus of praise. The Lord who has sent His people to the ends of the earth is worshiped by the believers who have come as a result of their witness.

John Stott reminds us that the Bible is the foundation for pursuing our commitment to the global cause of Christ with this summary:

Without the Bible, world evangelization is impossible. For without the Bible, we have no Gospel to take to the nations, no warrant to take it to them, no idea of how to set about the task, and no hope of any success. It is the Bible that gives us the mandate, the message, the model, and the power we need for world evangelization. So let us seek to repossess it by diligent study and meditation. Let's heed its summons, grasp its message, follow its directions, and trust its power. Let's lift up our voices and make it known.[6]

The Historical Precedent

When the first-century believers obeyed Christ's commission, they went out simply in obedience to His Word. We too have His Word as the foundation of our commitment, but we also have a second foundation stone: We are not alone.

The saints who have gone before us—both from biblical times and during the history of the church—give us impetus to persevere. We do not operate in isolation. We have what the writer of Hebrews called a "great cloud of witnesses" (Heb. 12:1) sitting in the heavenly grandstand cheering us on as we run our portion of the race for God's glory.[7]

Heroes from the past cheer us on. When we flag in our zeal, we can turn to William Borden of Yale. This heir to a family fortune sacrificed it all because of his commitment to the worldwide purposes of God. After donating thousands of dollars to the missionary endeavor, Borden went out as a member of the Student Volunteer Movement in an effort to reach Muslims. After only four months in Egypt, he contracted cerebral meningitis in Cairo and died at age twenty-five.

In spite of what appears to be a tragically premature death from a human vantage point, Borden cheers us on with his view of life, words inscribed in the flyleaf of his Bible:

NO RESERVE
NO RETREAT
NO REGRETS.

We find a courage from his example that urges us to continue without turning back.

In another section of that great grandstand sits Amy Carmichael, founder of the Dohnavur Fellowship in India. As we think of the pain we incur as we run the race of faith, she shouts out, "Hast thou no scar?" We remember her example of enduring great loneliness and physical burden in her last twenty years of ministry to temple prostitutes in India. We remember the poem in which she exhorts us with the voice of Jesus to persevere in spite of physical hardship:

But as the Master shall the servant be,
And pierced are the feet that follow me.
Can he have followed far
Who has no wound, no scar?

As we round another turn, we contemplate quitting the race again. This time we encounter Lott Carey, the first black missionary from North America. Here we meet a man who came out of a world that told him he was less than a human, but he listened to God, not men. He bought his freedom in 1813 and sailed to West Africa. Before departing, he spoke to his friends: "I am about to leave you; and expect to see your faces no more. I long to preach to the poor Africans the way of life and salvation. I don't know what may befall me, or whether I may find a grave in the ocean, or among the savage men, or more savage wild beasts, on the Coast of Africa; nor am I anxious what may become of me. I feel it my duty to go."[8]

Heroes of the present also provide motivation. Chet

Bitterman greets us with words of encouragement. This man reminds us of God's sovereign purposes, even through pain and hardship. An aspiring Wycliffe Bible translator, Bitterman desired to serve in Malaysia, but because of the need, he went instead to Colombia in 1981. Early in his time in Colombia, he was sent to the capital for gall bladder surgery. While awaiting surgery, he was mistakenly kidnapped by terrorists and held for forty-eight days before being shot through the heart. As a result of the highly publicized martyrdom of Bitterman, 200 new volunteers came forward to serve in Bible translation. His death illustrates God's bringing good out of evil (Gen. 50:15–21).

We gain courage by learning of Anglican Bishop Festo Kivengere of Uganda. In the face of the "wild man of Africa," the mad dictator Idi Amin, Kivengere stood and accused him of abusing his authority and warned him that he would be judged by God. Kivengere inspires us to stand boldly for the Lord, no matter what the opposition.

Floyd McClung and his family likewise provide an example that only the courageous can follow. In spite of the obvious dangers, Floyd and his wife, Sally, raised their family while doing urban ministry, first in Kabul, Afghanistan—reaching out to drug addicts and seekers on the "hippie trail"—and presently in Amsterdam, Netherlands—where they moved into an apartment building between the Church of Satan and a house of prostitution. They teach us how God works today even as He did with Daniel in the lion's den or David before Goliath—to protect His faithful people.[9]

Brian Stiller of the Evangelical Fellowship of Canada illustrated the dramatic impact of the saints who have gone before us by telling the story of a young American football player. This young man was, at best, an average player who spent most of his time sitting on the bench. Occasionally, the player would bring his father to watch games, and it always struck the coach that the father seemed to hang on his son when they walked away after the game.

One day the coach got word that the young man's father had died. He went to pay his respects, and to his surprise, the young player made a request: "Coach," he said, "will you grant me one wish?"

The coach, cautious not to hurt the already grieved young man said, "Well, sure, I'll try."

"Please let me start in the game tomorrow."

The coach did not know how to answer. He wanted to grant the grieving boy's request, but he knew it was an important game. Not wanting to go back on his word, however, he consented.

The game came, and the young man was sent in to play with the coach thinking, "I'll pull him back to the bench as soon as he starts making mistakes." To the coach's surprise, however, the young man played extraordinarily. He was everywhere on the field, executing tackles, making big plays, and exceeding any performance the coach had ever seen before in practice.

After the game, the coach approached the young man and asked, "What got into you today? I never expected you to do so well, especially after your father's death."

"But coach," the young man responded, "I played that well *because* of my father's death. You see, Coach, my father was blind, so this was the first game he ever saw me play."

The thought of his father in that great "cloud of witnesses" motivated him to do his best. As we too are inspired to action, because of the heroes of faith who have gone before us, we will be building our commitment to grow as world-class Christians on the second foundation stone—the saints.

Emotion Will Not Keep Us

The tragic story of Hank Gathers teaches us the power of

emotion. When we confront the realities of eternity and the death of millions of people without Christ, our emotions will be stirred.

But emotional response is limited. We cannot sustain our vision on emotion alone. Instead, we build our world-class vision, action, and commitment on facts:

• That the Almighty God, the Creator of the ends of the earth, has revealed Himself to be God of all people and nations, and He solicits our participation in bringing these people to understand His Gospel and His glory.

• That this God reveals Himself as the one true Saviour (Isa. 43:11) and that His primary revelation is through His Son, Jesus Christ. There is salvation found in no one else (Acts 4:12) because He is the way, the truth, and life by which all people must come to God (John 14:6). This unique Saviour must be proclaimed to a world without hope outside of Him.

• That we are not alone; a great cloud of witnesses has gone before us, and as we get to know their lives, we are motivated and encouraged to persevere ourselves.

Action Items
A solid world-class vision needs information. Here are four practical ways to build our information base about the Scriptures and the saints:

1. A book that provides a biblical overview of God's global mandate throughout the Scriptures is William Dyrness' *Let the Earth Rejoice!* (Westchester, Ill.: Crossway Books, 1983). It helps point the reader to all the worldwide implications throughout the Bible.

2. Another idea for helping get a well-rounded understanding of God's plan for the world would be to take a concordance and look up (over a period of days or weeks) all the verses that contain the words *world*, *earth*, or *nations*. There are many.

3. The idea of Jesus Christ being the only Saviour (and therefore all people without Him being lost) is tough to accept. To wrestle with this issue, look up John 14:6 or 1 Timothy 2:4, and then ask questions like, " How can people be saved without Jesus as their Saviour ?" or "If some can be saved without knowing Jesus Christ, then why did He need to come and die?" (Two helpful books here are J. Robertson McQuilkin's *The Great Omission* [Grand Rapids: Baker Books, 1985] and Don Richardson's *Eternity in Their Hearts* [Ventura, Calif.: Regal Books, 1981].)

4. *From Jerusalem to Irian Jaya* (Grand Rapids: Zondervan Publishing House, 1983) by Ruth Tucker is probably the finest tool available for understanding the work of God through the saints over the ages. With succinct, two to six page sketches, the reader meets the most notable personalities of 2,000 years of Christian mission. If you do not want to read the entire book, look in the "Illustration Index" and you will be directed to saints whose lives illustrate topics such as Christ-centeredness, endurance, reconciliation, sacrifice, and success.

INFORMATION
AND
ISSUES

*A world-class Christian lifestyle is compatible with
what God is doing in our world.*

Anthropologists identify the earliest stages of societies as
"hunters and gatherers," those people who foraged through
the fields and forests gathering berries and roots and other
edibles for their sustenance. I like to think of world-class
Christians as "hunters and gatherers" in a different way. To
further our growth, we are always hunting for information
and gathering data about issues in the world into which God
calls us. Building on the two-part foundation of the Scriptures
and the saints, we continue to grow by foraging through
books, newspapers, and a host of other sources to expand our
minds concerning God's great world.

Hunting for information and gathering data is a lifelong
challenge, so let's consider some of the habits of world-class
Christians.

Information
Do we live in a global village or not? While those who focus
their lives on missions continue to discuss the miniaturiza-
tion of our world, many seem to be increasingly ignorant

about the world and its affairs. It is almost as if the rich are getting richer (i.e., those whose jobs are global in nature continue to learn about intercultural issues, worldwide developments, and international economies) while the poor get poorer (i.e., those who are not required to learn about world issues diminish in their knowledge of what is happening around the globe).

Brian O'Connell cited an incident several years ago when sixteen candidates for a senatorial seat were given a "pop quiz" on current events. Of five questions, only one candidate answered more than two questions correctly. O'Connell concluded: "Unfortunately, this lack of knowledge among leaders reflects a lack of information and concern for international affairs among the bulk of our society. Almost without exception, polls show that Americans are uninformed and unconcerned about international events."[1]

Is this lack of knowledge any less among Christians? Happily, I have found that an increased desire to know God's purposes in the world is leading many Christians to grow in their concern for world events. Pastors include global issues in their pastoral prayers. Churches rise up to care for refugees in their area. Missionaries find increased interest in global issues when they bring their reports home, and international Christian leaders find themselves issuing challenges from many North American pulpits.

But we still have many opportunities to grow!

Gathering global information can help us continue to build a world-class Christian vision. Where to start? How about purchasing an up-to-date map? A missions committee asked me what they could do to expand their church's world vision. I suggested a world map in a prominent place in the foyer. One member proudly responded, "We already have one." I went to see it.

The huge map covered the wall facing the sanctuary. Everyone would see it when they walked in. That was the good news. The bad news? The map still had countries with names like Rhodesia, The Belgian Congo, and French Indo-China on it rather than Zimbabwe, Zaire, and Vietnam. Anyone who knew the modern world would look at this map and think, "This church has a world vision, but they are considerably out of date."

One school of business management, encouraging readers to "take global education seriously," wrote:

> American citizens may be among the world's most prosperous, but according to a recent *National Geographic* study conducted by the Gallup Poll, their geographical knowledge is hardly world-class. In the nine-nation survey of 10,820 adults, U.S. respondents finished third from the bottom. . . . Among the American respondents, 75 percent failed to locate the Persian Gulf on a map. At the same time, fewer than half could find the United Kingdom, France, South Africa, or Japan. Using blank maps, the average American could identify only four of twelve European nations, and fewer than six of ten U.S. states. Perhaps most humiliating, one in seven U.S. adults could not identify the United States on a map.[2]

Buy a map! Or better yet, how about a copy of Patrick Johnstone's *Operation World?* This international handbook for Christians outlines every country of the world over the course of 365 days, gives pertinent data, and then offers specific prayer requests for the country of the day. *Operation World* (which is updated about every three years) provides an excellent source of global information while helping us with our geography.

Knowing the world in which we live is essential for effective functioning as world-class Christians. Gilbert Grosvenor of the *National Geographic* warns, "Our adult population, especially our young adults, do not understand the world at a time in our history when we face a critical economic need to understand foreign consumers, markets, customs, opportunities, and responsibilities."[3]

Grosvenor's concern is economic. Our concern goes beyond that, since God calls us to be His ambassadors (2 Cor. 5:20). Ignorance of our world can discredit our witness. An international student from Peru told me of being introduced to an American who said, "Oh yes, Peru, the islands off the coast of Ecuador."

"No," the student politely replied, "You are thinking of the Galapagos Islands. Peru is the country directly below Ecuador."

"No, I think you are incorrect," the American replied belligerently, and the conversation came to an abrupt halt.

My Peruvian friend told me that the conversation was not ruined by the American's incorrect location of Peru. Many international people are tolerant of our geographic ignorance. "It was his arrogance, telling me that I did not know where my own country is." An opportunity lost as an "ambassador for Christ" because of arrogance added to geographic ignorance.

Reading can further our informational growth. A myriad of rich opportunities are available to us through the printed media. Larry, the chairman of our missions committee, is a self-taught missions specialist. By trade he is an electrician, but a unique situation in his job grants him some time to read. His global information gathering, unsurpassed in our church, includes missions periodicals, biographies, books about mission strategy, and even sections of David Barrett's mammoth work, *The World Christian Encyclopedia*. Larry stands as an example to us all that the information is out there if we are willing to discipline ourselves to read.

For some, disciplined reading comes only as a result of being in a structured learning situation. A course on international business, cross-cultural understanding, or even geography and history might serve as a catalyst for world-class learning. The "Perspectives" Course (out of the U.S. Center For World Mission), which provides an excellent overview of the world Christian movement, can stimulate any Christian to read and thus gain a broader understanding of our world.

World-class information gathering can also include reading the international section of the newspaper, catching excerpts of God's work around the world through publications from missions agencies, or consulting global reports such as *Church Around the World*[4] or those produced by the Evangelical Missions Informations Service.[5]

Radio, Television, and Movies can foster greater growth in our gathering of information. One friend listens to radio station HCJB out of Quito, Ecuador "simply to hear the Gospel going out in another language." Another listens to National Public Radio because it offers more in-depth reporting on international events (which may not even be covered by network news stations).

Cable Network News opens global horizons to us. Some grow by watching programs related to cultures, nature, or international events featured on PBS. *National Geographic* specials take us around the world, educating us and giving us fuel for global praying about people, cultures, and places that we may never see firsthand.

One friend collects videos about other parts of the world. *Out of Africa, Passage to India, Gandhi*, and others have some value in educating us about culture and history, and they can provide enjoyable ways for us to learn. *Chariots of Fire* offers us information and insight about the great missionary Eric Liddell.

In all this learning, the goal is not merely cognitive growth.

Instead, we seek out information so that we might be more effective "ambassadors for Christ" in the immediate world into which He sends us. One man, after hearing a radio report of testimonies from the Lausanne II Conference in Manila of the Gospel going forward in the face of hardship, wrote, "A report like that makes it easy for guys like me to go out into the marketplace during the week with motivation to present the Gospel with excitement."

What do missionaries do? Answering this question further stirs our knowledge of God at work in the world, but many of us need more contemporary answers. Past images of white, pith-helmeted missionaries carrying the Gospel to helpless savages desperately need updating. Cross-cultural workers now come from every continent and go to every continent. The Third World international ministry force will soon surpass the number of personnel from traditional "sending countries."

And not every cross-cultural worker plants churches. Some, working with relief and development ministries, plant plants. "Tentmakers" use business, teaching, medical, and engineering skills to gain access to countries that do not allow traditional missionaries. Some international "ambassadors of Christ" go as pioneers to primitive tribes working in inaccessible jungles, but many others go now as pioneers in modern cities working in urban jungles.

World-class information gathering means enlarging our vision of what is being done (and what remains to be done) by the international network of Christian workers in a variety of contexts and cultures.

One last word about information gathering: Make it fun! Learning about cultures might include an international meal. Studying the map does not require sitting in the library; instead, buy a world map beach ball and read it while getting a tan. My friend, Larry, does an enormous amount of reading, but this includes children's books—from picture books to coloring books to easy-to-read biographies like *My Book about Hudson* (about Hudson Taylor).

Expand your world knowledge, have some geographic fun by trying to decipher twelve capitals of Europe from these:[6]

1. LOBS IN   7. LEG BEARD
2. DID ARM   8. WAS RAW
3. SHIN-LIKE   9. CUB'S HEART
4. I SPAR   10. OPEN CHANGE
5. A TRAIN   11. HAS TEN
6. GEAR UP   12. NON-OLD

Issues
Hunting for international information coincides with gathering data pertaining to issues that threaten the spread of the Gospel. While there are hundreds of issues that any of us could focus upon, there are several "mega-issues" that we all should at least be aware of (and perhaps which every church should give at least partial consideration to during the course of the year).

Morris Watkins identifies some of these "mega-issues" in *Seven Worlds to Win*. He points out the greatest challenges facing the spread of worldwide Christianity as:

1. The Chinese world (one of every five people on earth)
2. The Hindu world (and the "New Age" carryover into the Western world)
3. The Buddhist world (much of South Asia)
4. The Muslim world (with a zeal to do its own brand of "evangelizing")
5. The Communist world (which is ever changing)
6. The Bibleless/illiterate world (over 3000 languages

yet to receive their own translation of the Bible and some countries with 95 percent illiteracy)
7. The So-Called Christian world (where Christianity is traditional but not personal).[7]

Floyd McClung and Kalafi Moala, in *Nine Worlds to Win*, include Watkins' "mega-issues" numbers 2, 3, 4, 5, and 7 and expand it further to include:

1. The world of the Poor and Needy (1 billion hungry people; thousands of slum neighborhoods around the world; 1 million street people in Calcutta)
2. The Urban world (with an estimated 75 percent of the world living in urban centers by the year 2010 and currently over 300 world-class cities (with populations exceeding 1 million)
3. The world of Youth and Children (over 35 percent of the Third World under age 15 and 50 percent under 25)
4. The Tribal world (many of the 12,000 "hidden peoples" with no access to the Gospel).[8]

Any list like these oversimplifies our world, but they provide a helpful tool to assist us in getting a grasp of the major issues facing the church around the world. Any one of these issues—or others that we may want to pursue, such as the staggering growth of the Third World missionary movement (people being sent from the non-Western world across cultures), or the AD2000 Movement (cooperative efforts to complete the task of world evangelization by the year 2000), or the remaining unreached peoples (12,000 distinct cultural groupings with no witnessing church in their midst)—can occupy us for the next decade, but a little information about each issue and specific information on one issue can help us to be acutely aware of the challenges ahead.

Implementation

Hunting for information and gathering data on issues—how can it be done? Any reasonable person could discount the above suggestions as unreasonable in light of the vast amount of information available.

But instead of getting overwhelmed, why not get started? Choose an issue, a country, a "hot-topic" in the world, a "people-group" and dive in:

1. Pray for God to start giving you opportunity to learn about your study topic. Several of our students started praying two years ago about Burkina Faso, West Africa. Suddenly they started noticing articles, seeing TV programs, and meeting people related to that tiny country. As they prayed, God opened new horizons of opportunity to learn.

2. Start clipping articles from the newspaper or news magazines and create your own files. I never realized how much was being written on Mozambique until several years ago, in preparation for a trip there, I started a file. Now it bulges with articles that help me understand and pray for the church in that country.

3. Go to the library and look up recent books (or, in *The Reader's Guide to Periodical Literature*, recent articles) on your topic. With so many events changing in our world, a trip to the library every one or two months is necessary, especially if our study topic is a "hot-spot" that is often in the news.

4. Utilize cross-cultural friends. When Nelson Mandela was released from jail in South Africa, I called some friends who live in Soweto (a township outside of Johannesburg) for a report. A phone call (costing about $10) gave me a firsthand report that was greater and more personal than any news broadcast.

5. Attend a seminar or lecture on your topic. Bill, a friend interested in China and especially Tibet, recently went to a lecture at a nearby college given by two scholars from Lhasa,

Tibet's capital. Cultural lectures at museums, libraries or colleges are often free of charge and provide excellent opportunities for questions.

6. Pool your information. A group studying massive issues like AIDS in Africa or hunger in Asia will accumulate much more information than any one individual—and the group learning can be stimulating and fun.

Look What God is Doing

The leaders at the Association of Church Missions Committees encourage world-class Christians to develop a bifocal vision:

- *nearsighted:* looking close at hand to the needs right around us, and
- *farsighted:* looking beyond ourselves to the world of need and opportunity outside of our normal sphere of influence.

Hunting for information and gathering data about global issues can add perspective to the world into which He calls us and power to our international prayers. As we forage through the stack of records of God at work in the world, we sing along with Scott Wesley Brown:

Look what God is doing
All across the land
See His Spirit moving
Feel His mighty hand
Breaking chains of darkness
Setting captives free
Look what God is doing
Through those who do believe
Glory Halleluia, look what God is doing

He is calling faithful men
To carry out His plan
So in the power of Jesus' name
Go possess the land
Take the living Gospel
Mix it with some love
Add a little action
And see what our God does
Glory Halleluia, look what God is doing![9]

Chapter Five

A LOOK AT
WORLD-CLASS
PRAYERS

The saint who advances on his knees never retreats.
Jim Elliot

Our team of fourteen arrived at the Moffatt College of Bible in Kijabe, Kenya almost two full days after we left home. We were safe and fairly rested, having endured two all-night flights, an all-day layover, two customs checks, and a variety of airplane food.

In contrast to other work teams that I had led, traveling with this one seemed almost too easy. The details, transfers, visa checkpoints, and a myriad of other loose ends that make up such a trip were flawlessly accomplished. Twenty-two pieces of luggage rolled off the belt, unscathed, in Nairobi, a miracle on any connecting flight.

When we introduced ourselves to the students at Moffat College, a student leader welcomed us: "For four months we have been praying for you every day, and now you are here. Welcome!"

In those words, we realized that our flawless travel was not due to my leadership or planning. We were on the receiving end of faithful, consistent prayer. We benefited because brothers and sisters who had never met us were faithful in prayer on our behalf. Our lives, travel, and safety had been touched, protected, and guided by our God in response to the prayers of people we did not know.

If we had any lofty thoughts of our coming to teach spiritual disciplines to these citizens of a Third World country, they dissipated in this welcome. We felt convicted by our own failure to pray. The students at Moffat College of Bible humbled us. But we also realized that God had worked through their prayers. In them, we saw the importance of prayer on a global scale. Because of the world-class nature of their prayers, our world was changed. Through them, we realized that prayer is our greatest asset for being a partner in God's work around the world. God wants to change the world, and He will do it through us and our prayers.

Biblical World-Class Prayers

The Bible introduces us to a host of men and women who lead the way in offering world-class prayers. None (except Jesus) were perfect, and several (David and Solomon) are as known to us because of their sins as their sanctification. Nonetheless, their prayers—saved by God forever in the Scriptures—give us a glimpse of the worship of God that extends far beyond cultural and geographic biases.

Consider Miriam, Moses' sister. Her prayer of worship and praise is recorded after the escape of the Israelites through the Red Sea. In Exodus 15:20-21, Miriam leads the people of Israel in a song to the Lord.

Her prayer focuses on God's victory. The Lord wins the battle. He throws the enemies into the sea. He defeats the greatest army in the world. He uses His power to overrule nature and achieve His purposes. All His enemies will fear because the God of Israel is the one true God. He will reign forever and ever.

Miriam's prayer is world-class because she points us to one of the greatest global themes in the Bible—God will win the victory. His kingdom will be established. He will defeat those that boast against Him, and He will lead His people into the final winner's circle, the message of the Book of Revelation.

Lucy exemplifies prayer in the spirit of Miriam. This faithful prayer champion attacks the most difficult issues of the day in her prayers. Recently, her focus has been the nation of Albania, the only atheist nation on earth. When Lucy prays, she prays with fervor but not panic. She knows that God will win the final victory, that the powers which oppose the Gospel now will fall just as the Pharoah's army was swallowed up in the Red Sea. Zeal without anxiety. Seriousness without worry. She knows that she is already on the winning team.

World-class prayer principle #1: God is the victor, the ultimate Lord of history. When we approach the topic of prayer for our world, we need to know that God is the winner. He is not worried. He will lead the church to final triumph, a triumph started through Jesus' death on the Cross and completed in His return.

Hannah exemplifies another world-class prayer. After struggling long and hard for God to answer her prayers for a child, God brings Samuel. Hannah dedicates him with her prayer in 1 Samuel 2:1-10. In spite of the fact that Hannah was probably uneducated, her prayer is remarkably articulate about the character of God as the Sovereign Judge of the earth:

The Lord brings death and makes alive;
He brings down to the grave and raises up.
The Lord sends poverty and wealth;
He humbles and He exalts.
He raises the poor from the dust

And lifts the needy from the ash heap;
He seats them with princes
And has them inherit a throne of honor.
The Lord will judge the ends of the earth
(1 Sam. 2:6-8, 10).

Hannah's prayer comes as great hope to any who suffer under the clutches of oppression. To us in the wealthier nations however, her prayer rebukes any self-satisfaction or self-reliance we might feel. We dare not enter into the world advancement of the church thinking that our wealth and success is somehow a result of our own doing. We are what we are because God has allowed it. Knowing the Sovereign Judge, who exalts one and puts down another, squelches our feelings of superiority toward any other people on earth.

Her prayer foreshadows the experience of King Nebuchadnezzar. In his power, opulence, and success, he deceived himself into thinking that he was self-sufficient: "Is this not the great Babylon I have built as the royal residence, by *my* mighty power and for the glory of *my* majesty?" (Dan. 4:30, emphasis mine). At such arrogance, God strikes Nebuchadnezzar down, reducing him to an animallike madman. Only when he comes to his senses and submits before God is he restored:

Then I praised the Most High; I honored and glorified
Him who lives forever:
His dominion is an everlasting dominion;
His kingdom endures from generation to generation.
All the peoples of the earth are regarded as nothing.
He does as He pleases with the powers of heaven and
the peoples of the earth.
No one can hold back His hand or say to Him, "What
have You done?"

(Dan. 4:34-35)

Nebuchadnezzar concludes, "And those who walk in pride He is able to humble" (Dan. 4:37).

World-class prayer principle #2: God is the Sovereign Judge; all that we have or are comes from His goodness and mercy. Nebuchadnezzar and Hannah remind any who possess power and wealth that these are given by the Sovereign Judge and must be used to His glory.

King David's prayers appear throughout the Old Testament, especially in the Psalms. His final prayer, however, is recorded in 2 Samuel 22:2-51, just before his death. David's prayer focuses on deliverance, on worshiping God because of His creative greatness, and on His faithfulness.

In the midst of this great prayer—just as David completes a hymn on God's awesome power in creation (verses 8-16)—he records one of the most profound personal truths in the Bible. "He reached down from on high and took hold of me" (v. 17). The Almighty God, the Creator of the ends of the earth, took ahold of me!

David points us to the great and awesome King of the Universe who takes an interest in us. He reminds us that in some mysterious way, the Sovereign Lord of all has divinely limited Himself to work through us.

World-class prayer principle #3: God is personal; He who rules the universe desires relationship with us. Of all the truths that thrust us forward into God's worldwide action, this is perhaps the greatest: GOD WANTS TO USE OUR LIVES! In the midst of worship, we realize that God has reached down to take hold of us through Jesus. When we understand this, we cannot help but join David in committing ourselves to praise Him among the nations (v. 50).

King Solomon, most famous for his wisdom and his temple, utilized both to offer an extraordinary prayer of dedication in

1 Kings 8:22-61. Realizing that God is not limited to this human structure (v. 27), Solomon still prays that his temple will be a place where God hears . . .

. . . to forgive

. . . to judge

. . . to save the foreigner.

In a world where most of Solomon's subjects were satisfied to hold the God of Israel as uniquely theirs, Solomon expands their vision through his prayer. He dedicates the temple that it may serve foreigners (non-Israelites) "so that all the peoples of the earth may know Your name and fear You" (v. 43) and "so that all the peoples of the earth may know that the Lord is God and there is no other" (v. 60).

World-class prayer principle #4: God hears and forgives so that His glory might be known in all the earth. In our world, where the Christian church is often content to build structures and programs which serve only the saved, we are wise to listen to Solomon. All that we do should be done to foster true worship of the Lord Most High — so that all the peoples of the world may know Him.

Daniel is our final Old Testament example. A true missionary in a pagan culture, Daniel faced a world that challenged his morals, his spirituality, and his convictions. Yet he endured under four kings as a wise and faithful voice for the Lord. One of his prayers illustrates at least one of the secrets of his staying power. Facing a baffling dream which no one could interpret, Daniel approaches the Lord as the giver of discernment. In Daniel 2:20-23, Daniel worships God as the giver of discernment, wisdom, power, and knowledge.

The mother of Hudson Taylor relied on God for discernment in a similar way. While struggling with frustration over the unconverted state of her teenage son, she, like modern parents, knew of no solution. She devoted herself to prayer, and over one two week period of separation from her family, she sensed the Lord leading her to pray faithfully for his salvation. She prayed until she was certain God had answered her.

When she returned home, her son reported to her of his personal conversion after reading Gospel tracts. God, the giver of discernment, led Mrs. Taylor to pray while He worked in the heart of her young son, who would become the greatest missionary pioneer of the nineteenth century.

Daniel and Mrs. Taylor illustrate a resolve to pray over issues which concern us. In our times, when we convince ourselves that we must spend our energies figuring things out and taking action, perhaps we would do better if we went first to God and asked for discernment.

World-class prayer principle #5: God gives discernment; He opens our minds to understand the times in which we live so that we can respond wisely. As we approach a world that baffles us, Daniel gives us a clue as to the priority of praying for discernment. Acknowledging that the signs of our times are too troubling for us to understand, we can come confidently before God asking Him to reveal the "deep and hidden things."

Jesus, in the New Testament, instructs us to pray, "Your kingdom come, Your will be done on earth as it is in heaven" (Matt. 6:10). His priority in prayer is God's will being done on earth.

This priority resulted in Jesus' call to die. When facing His final betrayal into the hands of His enemies, Jesus offers His greatest prayer (John 17). In spite of the personal suffering that lay ahead, Jesus prays for His disciples and all that would come after them (including us). His prayer focuses directly on God's kingdom being declared on earth. He prays for Christians to be one "to let the world know that You sent Me and have loved them even as You have loved Me" (John 17:23).

In other words, Jesus prays not for His own safety or success. Instead, He prays for the unity of Christians so that the world might know the Gospel. He demonstrates to us that our prayers should not be anchored to our personal concerns but should go beyond these to the spread of the Gospel. Even when it involves personal discomfort, the coming of the kingdom through the united body of Christ is our priority concern.

Mrs. Josephine Kennedy began praying in the late 1940s for God to raise up a witness to Himself in the northwestern suburbs of Boston. She cared only for Christ to be exalted, and for several years, she alone carried this ministry of prayer. Mrs. Kennedy prayed for a group of believers, unified around Jesus Christ and committed to His worldwide commission, to be raised up.

By the early fifties, others joined her in prayer. They believed that God wanted to raise up a church in their community of Lexington. They formed a fellowship group and, in faith, they laid aside some denominational nuances to form an interdenominational church. Steps of faith, prayer, and an outward focus on witness and missions prevailed.

Over forty years later, Mrs. Kennedy's prayers continue to be answered. The church that God raised up in answer to her prayers has grown to over 2000 members, 70 missionaries working in 30 countries, and an active witness in the local community and the Boston area. Following her spirit and the spirit of Christ in John 17, Grace Chapel still chooses not to be divided over issues that often divide churches (eschatology, the charismatic movement, etc.) but unites together around the centrality of declaring Christ to the world.

World-class prayer principle #6: Jesus' kingdom and the united action of believers should take precedence over our own personal issues. Will we pray for the spread of the Gospel in our area, even if God answers our prayer by granting growth to the church down the street? Will we go beyond our own needs and pray for those whose needs make ours look insignificant? Will we pray for other Christian groups to be successful, even though we may disagree with some of their doctrinal positions?

The Apostle Paul offers one more world-class example of prayer. In Ephesians 1:15-23 and then in the great benediction of Ephesians 3:20-21, Paul lifts our eyes upward to see the greatness of God. Hope in Him motivates us to carry on. The great assignment of declaring His glory is made possible because of His power.

When we come to the challenge of world evangelization with the realization that Jesus is the beginning and the end of what we do, we cannot help but join Paul in worshiping Him who is able to do "immeasurably more than all we ask or imagine" (Eph. 3:21).

In the late 1940s and early 1950s, God called out many who would pray Ephesians 1:15-23 prayers for the estimated 1 million Chinese Christians who were left without missionaries or foreign helpers after Mao Tse-Tung came to power. The Peoples Republic of China stands today as a testimony of God changing the world through prayer. Those who were ousted "left China on their knees and never got up. They left physically but never spiritually."[1] Carl Lawrence pays tribute to these people of world-changing prayer:

They were not defeated; they simply continued to do battle in one of the toughest arenas of all: intercessory prayer. They were often maligned for not realizing that this was a "different world we live in, and there is nothing you can do for China." Few were (or have been) recognized for their contribution to the building of His kingdom. They nevertheless continued hour by hour, day by day, and year by year, remembering by name those they left behind in the villages and communities that spread across China. Their work was far beyond any job description which man might design.[2]

Without exaggeration, those that committed themselves to pray for China experienced "more than they could ask or imagine" when the doors to China began to reopen in the 1970s. Reports came out that the church of 1 million had grown to over 50 million. Today, some report even higher figures. China is a remarkable testimony to the power of the Holy Spirit to bring "glory in the church and in Christ Jesus throughout all generations, forever and ever!" (Eph. 2:21)

World-class prayer principle #7: Expectation. When we pray for ourselves and other believers around the world, we do so with the anticipation that God will act mightily so that all may "know the hope to which He has called you, the riches of His glorious inheritance in the saints, and His incomparably great power for us who believe" (Eph. 1:18-19).

Others in the Scriptures offer prayers which instruct us about praying with an enlarged worldview. These are a few select examples. They teach us not only how to grow in prayer but also that God is the starting point of prayer. Their example of prayer shows that a majority of their attention focused on some aspect of the character of God, and from that vantage point of worship, their view of the world was changed. The same will happen for us when we focus on who God is and allow our prayers to flow from this vision.

Why Prayer?

All of us would like to be part of changing the world, but prayer seems so docile. Why not dedicate ourselves to *ac-*

tion? Why spend time cultivating and building the discipline of prayer?

The task is too big for us! If accumulating world information does not overwhelm us, the needs of people certainly will. Some will be overcome by emotion while others retreat from an acute sense of guilt. All of it leads to one basic conclusion: We cannot accomplish God's purposes in our own strength.

When Jesus saw the crowds as "harassed and helpless, like sheep without a shepherd" (Matt. 9:36), He did not command His disciples to run around in frenzied activity trying to meet all the needs. He commanded them to pray (Matt. 9:38) that the Lord of the harvest would act.

We need to pray keeping in focus the fact that Jesus is the Lord of this harvest. Harassed and helpless people will overwhelm us if we are not hearing first from the Commander who sends us out. Tom Wells explains the priority of prayer: "Prayer is our first work in the harvest. And the reason is not hard to find. It is this: the harvest has a 'Lord'. He oversees the harvest. Someone supplies the workers. Someone controls the progress. And that 'Someone' is God. *Our first business is not to look at the size of the harvest. Our first business is to pray to our God"[3]* (emphasis mine).

God uses prayer to mold us. Sometimes we come to prayer in an effort to change God's mind. By contrast, the biblical concept of prayer includes waiting on God so that He can change our wills to His will. God used three days in the belly of a fish to change Jonah's mind about obeying Him and going to Nineveh. In the time of prayer (what else could Jonah do?) God molded Jonah's will to His own will.

As we pray, God will change our thoughts, dreams, plans, and prayers. Missionaries often start their stories by saying, "When I first became a Christian, the last thought in my mind was becoming a missionary." But, over time, growth, and prayer, God changed their minds. He used prayer to change priorities, reorient values, and alter plans.

A friend in inner-city ministry told me of the effect of prayer in his own life. He grew up in a church where subtle racism pervaded the missions emphasis. Jokes about people being poor "because they were lazy" were common. The insinuation that non-whites were somehow inherently inferior to whites affected his perspective as a young Christian. He finally sensed God calling him to cross-cultural ministry, and with a genuine desire to help "these poor black folks" out, he started to prepare. Preparation included prayer.

As he prayed, God began to change him. He read in the Scriptures about Samaritans and Gentiles and poor and widows. He began to realize that the attitudes he had grown up with were sinful and destructive to the personal worth of those he was going to serve. The Holy Spirit convicted him of his racism, identified pride, and gave him grace to repent. When he finally went to the city, his spirit had been transformed so that he could go as a servant, not a condescending leader.

When Jesus commands us to pray for our enemies, perhaps He is using our submission to Him in prayer as one way in which our attitudes might be changed. When we open ourselves before God in prayer, He can do a ministry of the Spirit to change hate into love, racial stereotypes into sacrificial service, or bitterness into blessing.

Prayer engages us in spiritual warfare. Jim Reapsome, the editor of the *Evangelical Missions Quarterly*, recently completed a study of the missions efforts headed toward the year 2000. In this study, he pointed out the obstacles that could hinder the accomplishment of the Great Commission. Sadly, the first reason he cited is the church itself. Within the church, the first problem he detected is "prayerlessness."

He wrote, "Missionary praying tends to be both too general and superficial, rather than specific and thorough." He went on to address the issue of spiritual warfare: "How can the barriers of Islam, Marxism, Hinduism, and Buddhism be broken down without prevailing, persistent prayer?"[4]

The Bible states that "we are not contending against flesh and blood, but against the principalities, against the powers, against the world rulers of this present darkness, against the spiritual hosts of wickedness in the heavenly places" (Eph. 6:12, RSV). How can we hope to be world-changers without prayer?

Be A World-Changer: Pray!

The *Reader's Digest* often includes sidebars with fascinating quotes or statistics. This one caught my eye: "Pounds of plutonium and highly enriched uranium that are unaccounted for in U.S. inventories: 9600. Pounds of plutonium needed to make an atomic bomb: 15."[5]

The point? There is a vast (and dangerous) amount of atomic bomb energy unaccounted for. The pounds of plutonium are out there — let's hope no one figures out how to tap the power for evil purposes.

The illustration made me think of the positive power available to us in prayer. A column in the *Heavenly Digest* might read: "Power to affect the world available through prayer: unlimited. World-class prayers being tapped: 15." God has given us access to His throne through prayer; He gives us the privilege to ask Him to do beyond anything we can ask or think. But only a few tap into the power.

Through worship and intercession, we engage the Lord of the harvest. By our petitions, we can be part of His work around the world. Wesley Duewel, author of *Touch the World Through Prayer*, suggests four ways that prayer involves us strategically in God's work around the world:[6]

1. Through prayer we can join any team that God is using. We can join in the efforts of missionaries in the Amazon

River Valley, in the ministries of pastors in Sri Lanka, or in the evangelistic efforts of "tentmakers" in North Africa!

2. Our prayers can water the harvest. Literature distribution or radio broadcasts can sow the seed of the Gospel, but we need to water this seed through our prayers.

3. Our prayers can cultivate the harvest. Many who do convert to Christ do so at the risk of their lives; we can be partners with these new believers—even as those who prayed for Chinese Christians in China after 1950—through intercession on their behalf.

4. Our prayers can influence world leaders. We can change leaders and governments as we pray for them to be used by God to foster the spread of the Gospel.

Dr. J. Christy Wilson is a world-changer through prayer. As a missionary in Afghanistan, he confronted the spiritual warfare of Islam directly. Now, as professor of missions and Dean of the Chapel at Gordon-Conwell Theological Seminary, he plays a part in God's worldwide ministry through his prayers. He has had a powerful impact in the lives of countless students (myself included!) because of his intercession on their behalf. His perseverance in prayer (praying regularly—by name—for each member of the student body and their families) has left an indelible imprint on students who have graduated to go into ministries all over the world.

What an opportunity we have to go to God in prayer and beseech Him—not only that He would make us like His Son, but that He will work mightily in the world! God invites us to be part of changing the world through prayer . . . How will you respond?

Chapter Six

OUR PRAYERS CAN BE WORLD-CLASS

Satan laughs at our toiling, mocks our wisdom,
but trembles when we pray.
The Kneeling Christian

My wife and I sat with missionaries in Mozambique, the civil war-ravaged country in southeast Africa. We listened to their accounts of difficulties with distributing food and clothing to people in desperate need. They sadly described the agony of thousands of people living on the edge of survival.

As they talked, a wave of helplessness overcame us. What could we possibly do? I asked the relief workers, "After we return home, is there anything we can do for you?"

They responded immediately: "Tell the people back home that we are depending on their prayers! We need God's supernatural help to continue this work."

Their answer reminded me of Paul's words to the Corinthians in the face of great persecution and hardship. He wrote of his hope in God's provision, but noted their human responsibility by stating, "On Him [God] we have set our hope that He will continue to deliver us, *as you help us by your prayers*" (2 Cor. 1:10-11, emphasis mine).

We can join God's worldwide team—helping others by our prayers—in the endeavor of communicating the Gospel of

Jesus Christ through word and deed.

We all have the incredible opportunity of participating in God's work worldwide, so why don't we? Let's consider three of the largest prayer obstacles and some ideas on how to respond to them:

Obstacle #1: *"It's too overwhelming"*
Response #1: *Pray manageably.*

All of us can be overtaken by a similar wave of helplessness—like the one that we felt in Mozambique—but we cannot succumb to the temptation to quit. The answer lies in manageable praying. I cannot pray for millions of hurting children in our world; I have difficulty focusing on Kenya, a country where 60 percent of the population is under age fourteen. But I can pray consistently for Oyie Kimasisa, the young Kenyan boy we support with World Vision. Using updates and reminders I receive from their Kenya office, I can participate in a ministry to Oyie through prayer. By concentrating on one child, I can manage my response in prayer.

When I asked a missionary the greatest way we (in a sending church) can encourage him, he responded immediately, "If one person in the church approached me and said, 'I have been praying for you every day,' I think I would start walking on air!" This missionary asked only that one person make it their manageable task to pray for him.

We can likewise pray manageably about world events. When the news reports a devastating earthquake, typhoon, or other natural disaster, manageable praying means lofting a "prayer arrow" (see p. 76)—a brief prayer that we can breathe to God about the crisis. We might pray for government leaders, relief coordinators, or local church leaders—that God will guide their efforts in responding. Through a brief and manageable prayer, we can be involved in that event.

Obstacle #2: *"But what do I pray about?"*
Response #2: *Pray practically.*

We err when we think that prayer is limited to eloquent oratory in King James English. We worship the Lord who taught us to pray for our daily bread. He welcomes our practical requests.

When we pray around the world, we often lack for specifics, so we need to use our imaginations. I have started developing "ever-widening circle" praying. I start with that which I know and then move outward, letting God direct my prayers.

I might start by praying for David and Stephanie Robinson, who direct a relief and development work in a north African country. I know them and their family, so I begin by praying for needs I am aware of. Then I move outward. I might pray (as God guides my imagination):

● that they will have success that day in meetings with government officials;

● that food distribution projects will not be blocked physically by sandstorms or administratively by red tape;

● or that well-drilling projects in that country will be successful on the first attempt.

Praying in these ever-widening circles can lead us to pray by God's direction for needs that we otherwise might never know about.

Obstacle #3: *"But will it make any difference?"*
Response #3: *Pray strategically.*

Our prayers do make a difference; God promises to work through them, and many people — like our friends in Mozambique — depend on the prayers of others.

To insure the maximum effectiveness in our prayers, we pray strategically. As the Bible commands, we pray first for "kings and all those in authority" (1 Tim. 2:2), because these leaders hold the keys to the work of the Gospel going forth.

We might pray for government leaders to accelerate the efforts of a development project. Or we could ask God to work even through communist leaders so that they will open the way for organizations like the English Language Institute to bring the Gospel through teachers in countries like Mongolia.

Strategic praying also calls us to pray for Christian leaders who guide the efforts of Christian work in their nations—like Dr. Theodore Williams in South India, Claude Noel in Haiti, Ajith Fernando in Sri Lanka, or Beatrice Zapata in Guatemala. (If you would like to pray for specific Christian leaders around the world, write to World Evangelical Fellowship P.O. Box WEF, Wheaton, IL 60189 for suggestions.)

Join God's Worldwide Team—Pray!

Paul wrote about Epaphras in his letter to the Colossians. Epaphras distinguished himself because he was "always wrestling in prayer" for those Colossian believers (Col. 4:12).

We can be like Epaphras, wrestling in prayer for people we may never meet or about needs to which we cannot personally respond. Through prayer we have the privilege and opportunity to touch our world.

David Howard, the general director of the World Evangelical Fellowship, shared some world-class praying in his book, *The Great Commission for Today*.

Howard was a missionary in Colombia, South America, where God seemed to be answering many prayers. There were new believers everywhere, and God was mightily at work.

At the same time, Dave's older brother, Phil, toiled among the Slavey Indians in Canada's Northwest Territories. Phil had worked with these Indians fourteen years without one convert.

In a prayer meeting with the Indians of his village, Dave shared his concern for his brother Phil. The village leader rose and invited the people to pray. Dave described what happened: "He didn't have to repeat the invitation. Two hundred people went to their knees immediately and began to pray. Their custom is for all to pray out loud together. . . . That evening they prayed for one hour and fifteen minutes without stopping. They poured out their hearts for Phil, his wife, Margaret, and for those Slavey Indians."[1]

The Colombian Indians' concern for Phil continued long after that prayer session. They sent letters to encourage him and persevered in prayer. David Howard found out later that Phil, after fourteen years of seemingly fruitless ministry, had reached an all-time low. He thought, "What's the use?" and wondered why he should continue. One night he went to bed defeated and discouraged; the next day he awoke with a new joy and courage to continue the work to which God had called him.

When the brothers compared dates, the times coincided exactly: The very night that Phil went to bed ready to quit and awoke revived was the night that those Colombian Indians had spent time in zealous prayer on his behalf.

We can wrestle in prayer as part of our partnership in the worldwide body of Christ. Whether we pray regularly for the ongoing work of a development project in Bangladesh, or for one child in Kenya, or loft a prayer arrow for evangelistic efforts in Soviet Armenia, we are essential parts of God's team.

Building Our Global Praying: 10 Steps To Get Started
Step 1: Start Where We Are and Build.[2] If we have never prayed for a missionary, the church in other countries, or leaders in foreign governments, let's get started! But don't be overwhelmed at the beginning by adding 168 countries or 35 missionaries all at once. If we are praying for no one in another land now, we can start by adding one person. When

this becomes established in our discipline of praying, we can add others later.

At our church, we publish a prayer calendar to help keep the international ministry family before the congregation. After the first edition, a zealous supporter of prayer and missions asked, "Why do you have only two pictures per month?" (He had hoped that we would have at least ten to twelve each month.) I explained, "If we had so many pictures that casual observers felt overwhelmed, what good would that do? We are trying to reach people who are just getting started, and two people are easier to pray for than ten."

We can all start small. There are 46,000 or more North American missionaries. Experts talk of over three times that number from Third World sending countries by the year 2000. I cannot fathom those numbers. But I can handle one or two.

Step 2: Practice Prayer Arrows. The biblical mandate to "pray without ceasing" (1 Thes. 5:17, NASB) requires us to try to live in an attitude of prayer. This attitude can include the lofting of prayer arrows—short prayers offered on the run or in response to an immediate need. Very few of us can pray for all of the countries of the world, but we can launch a prayer arrow for a country that we hear about in the news, an international worker that pops to our mind while we are driving, or a national church that is facing unusual challenges.

I use any means available to help me pray around the world. The other day, I put on a shirt and noticed that the label read, "Assembled in Mauritius." I stopped to offer an arrow prayer for the church in Mauritius, those that work there as missionaries, and the spiritual challenges they face. Then I realized how little I knew about Mauritius, so the next day, I got my copy of *Operation World* and learned about more specific ways to pray for that island nation.

Other catalysts for arrow prayers might include the labels on bananas (which often identify the country where the bananas were harvested), names of companies that provoke world-class thoughts (like "Global Van Lines"), or reading the "Arrivals/Departures" screen while waiting to pick someone up at the airport.

Step 3: Fuel Prayer with Information. The generic "bless the missionaries" or "guide the church around the world" prayers are far too expansive. We need information about specific people and places to help our prayers. The resources like Operation Mobilization Prayer Cards (see resources) or *The Church Around the World* (mentioned earlier) provide helpful facts to get us started.

A missionary family in Kenya told me that they were chagrined to return home on one furlough and hear that people had been praying for their protection from leopards. The missionary responded, "We have been in Kenya eighteen years, and we have prayed to see a leopard without success. In all, our years in East Africa, we have never heard of one missionary being attacked by a leopard. Instead, dozens of our friends have been injured or killed in car accidents. We need people to pray about the real dangers we face—like the highways!"

Prayer letters, international missions periodicals, or direct contact with those working overseas can provide the fuel we need for intelligent, accurate praying. When we pray for our friends in Quito, Ecuador, our first inclination is to think, "They live on the equator in South America; therefore, I will pray for God to give them grace to withstand the high heat and tropical humidity." A little information changes our prayer; after we find out that Quito (at 9000 feet) has year-round daytime temperatures of 70 degrees and nighttime temperatures of 55, we pray, "God, help us not to be jealous of our friends' weather in Quito!"

Step 4: Pray as Part of Our Correspondence. The New Testament Epistles include some excellent prayers on behalf of churches or individuals. Paul prayed for these churches as he wrote. We can do the same as we develop our ministry of correspondence and encouragement with missionaries and friends from other countries. As we write to them, we can let the Holy Spirit teach us how to pray for them.

Bob Hill, a teacher at Greater Europe Mission's Greek Bible Institute in Athens, suggests combining prayer and correspondence: "Keep track of missionaries' current prayer needs and find out what requests have been answered. If you have been praying about something daily for several months, write to ask how the Lord is working with regards to the subject. Ask about special needs. Some items cannot be shared with the general public, and your missionary will appreciate your praying for these needs as well."[3]

Step 5: Participate in the Team Effort of Prayer. While individual intercession is a necessary discipline, group prayer is a powerful tool of God to guide the participants in "agreeing together" (Matt. 18:19). Groups like Concerts of Prayer, the Frontier Fellowship (see resources) or other mission-agency sponsored groups can encourage global intercession.

I am ashamed of the number of times I have told people I would pray for them and then forgotten. Corporate prayer helps me grow in faithfulness. Joining together with other brothers and sisters in Christ helps me face the magnitude of the task because I share the intercession with them.

Dr. Stanley Allaby, pastor of the Black Rock Congregational Church in Connecticut, told a seminar of church mission leaders how he became convinced of the need for faithful, corporate prayer for the missions family. "Early in my ministry," he said, "we sent out our church's first 'home-grown' missionaries. This family was the pride of our missions department.

"After their first term was over, they returned to our church for a year. At the close of the year, I asked the husband, 'So, Phil, when will you be heading back overseas?'

"Phil responded, 'Pastor, I'm not sure we're going back.'

"Why not?' I responded.

" 'Well, Pastor, after a year here at the church, I am just not convinced that the church has been and will be praying for us.' "

Allaby went on to describe his own personal repentance and his commitment to lead the church in corporate prayer on behalf of the international family that they had sent out. "Through the honesty of that missionary," Allaby concluded, "I became convinced that we must be true to our commitments because our missionary family is depending on us."

Step 6: Find a Personal Plan. When I am inspired to build the discipline of prayer in my own life, I am tempted to copy the person who has motivated me. If sixteenth century reformer Martin Luther rose at 4 A.M. to pray, then I want to do the same. Imitation is a great learning tool, but we must develop our own patterns for effective prayer. Some will pray well as they jog; others need complete silence. A few will like the idea of all-night vigils once per month. Others do better with fifteen consistent minutes every day. We need to find a plan that works for our lifestyle, metabolism, and spiritual maturity.

One student told me that his prayers for the world Christian movement became consistent when he put a map of the world on the ceiling over his bed. "When I first awake, the map reminds me to pray for the world—starting with the world into which I am sent, but extending beyond my friends to people I pray for in other countries."

The folks at the Caleb Project advocate a prayer plan that moves from the broadest topics to the most specific. In pray-

ing for Muslims in New Delhi, India, they start with prayer at
the *macro level* (Muslims worldwide). Then they progress
inward, praying at the *country level* (India), at the *city level*
(New Delhi), the *people level* (Muslims as opposed to Hindus),
the *church level* (for the evangelistic efforts of the Indian
church), at the *laborer level* (for specific Indian Christians who
are trying to reach these Muslims), and finally at the *personal
level* (how does God want me to respond personally?).[4]

Step 7: Choose Appropriate Tools. Prayer should never be mechanical, but there are tools that can increase our effectiveness in prayer. The tools that we choose might be prayer
cards of specific missionaries, maps, or prayer guides like the
Frontier Fellowship guide. We may also want to think of our
prayer posture as a tool. Some of us will choose to intercede
in a kneeling posture beside a bed or chair. Others will
choose to stand or sit.

During a recent bout with sleeplessness, I tried a new
tool—praying through the alphabet around the world. One
night I focused on cross-cultural workers I knew whose last
names began with A through Z. I got stuck on X (so I prayed
for missionaries who followed the example of Francis Xavier
by going to serve in East Asia), but in general, it was a
productive prayer time, much more useful than counting
sheep.

Another night I decided to pray for countries: Algeria, Bel-
gium, Chad, Dominica, Egypt, etc. The stumpers? Q is limited to Qatar (although I added a prayer for Quito, Ecuador). Z
seemed tough, until I remembered places in Africa—Zambia,
Zimbabwe, Zaire, and even Zanzibar and Zululand. The toughest again was X; I could not come up with anything, so in the
morning I looked in a missions dictionary. In the future, I will
remember the Xhosa people of South Africa when I pray
around the geographical alphabet.

Step 8: Remember to Intercede. The Pauline prayers from his letters to the Colossians or Philippians should guide our intercession. Effective global intercession will mean prayer for spiritual growth, victory in spiritual warfare, and effectiveness in the face of opposition for brothers and sisters around the world. If our petitions are superficial or preoccupied with physical needs, we may never experience the power of answered prayer.

Carl, a missionary in South America for twenty years, lamented after a furlough visit home, "In multiple visits with all of my supporting churches, no one has asked me about my spiritual health, and when I came home last June, my spiritual life was in a state of disrepair. I wasn't praying, my Scripture reading had lapsed, and I was thinking of quitting the ministry. People should never think that because I am a missionary, I am automatically spiritual."

Carl makes a valid point. People who serve in "professional" ministry need prayer for faithfulness in Bible reading, diligence in witnessing, and perseverance in praying. In other words, interceding effectively means praying for them about the same spiritual struggles that we encounter on a daily basis.

Step 9: Pray by Faith (Not by Results). The church in China, the Gospel's advance in Muslim countries, and the growth of Christians in little-known areas such as Albania, North Korea, or Mongolia compel us to pray by faith. We commit these places and believers to the Lord—believing that He is at work, even when we do not see it!

In 1983, my wife and I took our first trip to East Africa. We experienced some of the results of the great East African revival as we met many men and women who were training for church leadership. In spite of the breakthroughs, however, we sensed a burden to pray for the Maasai people who—

at that point—had still been quite resistant to the Gospel. Without much information, but with hope, we continued.

In 1988, we began to hear of some breakthroughs, and in 1989, I had the privilege of meeting Mary, a Maasai Christian who served as a schoolteacher. She shared the movement of the Holy Spirit in bringing many Maasai to Jesus Christ.

For Christie and me, it was a lesson in faith—praying for five years concerning people we scarcely knew. But God demonstrated His faithfulness in response to our prayers and the prayers of thousands of others for the Maasai. We remembered to pray at the urge of God's Spirit and not by tangible results.

Step 10: Learn to Say No. If we are to be effective in our intercession, we must learn to live within our own limitations of time and concentration ability. As we pray globally, we will find ourselves besieged with requests to pray more. If we are to be faithful in the priorities that we sense from God, we will need to say no. Most of us cannot pray for thousands of people by name or even hundreds of geographic areas. We need to learn to say no so that we continue to be faithful intercessors in a few areas. In general, faithfulness in prayer leads to fruitfulness in ministry; failure in prayer (committing ourselves to pray for too many people or needs) leads to frustration.

A man called me and asked for a meeting. He wanted to explain his ministry to me in hopes that our church could support him financially. I told him that we had no finances available. He responded, "Well, brother, could I come meet with you so that you could be on my prayer team?" Earlier in my life, I would have said yes simply out of guilt. But I was just learning this principle of saying no to unrealistic demands. I responded, "Brother, I must tell you the truth. If you came to meet with me, I would pray for you here in my office, but probably not again. I have joined the prayer team of many international workers, and I know I am not faithful in praying for them, so I must say no to your invitation to be on your team." He was miffed at my honesty, but I determined that I must say no rather than lie by pretending I would pray for him as he had asked.

A Worldwide Ministry

Friends in Mozambique asked us to tell the people in our church that they depended on their prayers. The Apostle Paul faced turmoil and opposition with confidence because he counted on the Corinthian believers to help him by their prayers.

We face the awesome challenge of helping others in their mission work around the world by supporting them through our prayers. Somewhere in the world, fellow Christians depend on our prayer partnership. Let's do our part to get the job done.[5]

Chapter Seven

A CHANGE
IN
LIFESTYLE

*A world-class Christian life-style is credible in
light of what God wants to do in our world.*

Judith Viorst has entertained both children and adults for
almost two decades through *Alexander and the Terrible, Horrible, No Good, Very Bad Day*. At some time or other, we all
identify with poor Alexander as he goes through a difficult
day dealing with gum in his hair, failure in school, the loss of
a best friend, a dessert-less lunch, a cavity, a fall in the mud,
and lima beans for dinner. The terrible, horrible, no good,
very bad day concludes with Alexander lamenting:

"There was kissing on TV and I hate kissing.

"My bath was too hot, I got soap in my eyes, my marble
went down the drain, and I had to wear my railroad-train
pajamas. I hate my railroad-train pajamas.

"When I went to bed Nick took back the pillow he said I
could keep, and the Mickey Mouse night-light burned out,
and I bit my tongue.

"The cat wants to sleep with Anthony, not with me.

"It has been a terrible, horrible, no good, very bad day."[1]

We laugh at Alexander. We identify with him, knowing

what it is like to have a day where nothing seems to go right. We see ourselves in his self-pity which exaggerates lima beans into a reason to move to Australia.

But the repeated theme in the book stimulates a nerve in the world-class Christian. As we laugh our way through Alexander's day, we suddenly hear the title repeated—not for Alexander, but for millions of others in our world who we know about through our research, outreach, and prayers.

There are millions of people in our world for whom every day is a terrible, horrible, no good, very bad day. One billion or more people go to bed hungry every evening. Thousands inhabit refugee camps where each day might bring a new disease, intensified suffering, or starvation. Millions live in squalor in our world's cities, some in houses made of cardboard boxes or sheets of aluminum and others scavenging through city dumps in an effort to stay alive.

Our knowledge makes us responsible. As soon as we read about or see these people—for whom every day is terrible, horrible, no good, very bad—we remember verses studied earlier. We ask ourselves, "What does John mean in this context: 'If anyone has material possessions and sees his brother in need but has no pity on him, how can the love of God be in him?' " (1 John 3:17) or what do we do with James' words: "Suppose a brother or sister is without clothes and daily food. If one of you says to him, 'Go, I wish you well; keep warm and well fed,' but does nothing about his physical needs, what good is it? In the same way, faith, by itself, if it is not accompanied by action, is dead"? (James 2:15-17)

These verses plus our knowledge of worldwide needs usually lead to guilt, and guilt, according to Bob Seiple of World Vision International, "is a paralytic emotion." In other words, we feel it, but it leads to inaction. We turn the TV off. We throw the mailing away. Or we react sarcastically, "So what am I supposed to do, send my leftovers to Manila?"

The Biblical Perspective

The combination of our relative affluence (on a global scale) with the awareness of world needs calls for some sort of action, and the Scriptures guide our efforts. While a few are called to complete abandonment of riches, all of us are called to stewardship, sacrifice, and solidarity. Let's take a closer look at these three.

(1) Stewardship: understanding that all that we have or are is God's already, and that He has assigned us responsibility as caretakers of His wealth. Paul wrote to Timothy about this stewardship perspective: "Command those who are rich in this present world not to be arrogant nor to put their hope in wealth, which is so uncertain, but to put their hope in God, who richly provides everything for our enjoyment. Command them to do good, be rich in good deeds, and to be generous and willing to share. In this way they will lay up treasure for themselves as a firm foundation for the coming age, so that they may take hold of the life that is truly life" (1 Tim. 6:17-19).

Tell the rich people to invest their riches in eternity. Putting hope in wealth makes us think that somehow we can "take it with us." Stewardship is the management of God-given resources in this life for which we will give an account in the next.

(2) Sacrifice: giving away something that costs us. Generosity gives out of abundance, but sacrifice gives when it hurts. Zaccheus (Luke 19) demonstrated generosity, but the widow who gave her last few cents (Luke 21) demonstrated sacrifice.

The Bible encourages a lifestyle of sacrifice. Killing the lamb without spot or blemish meant sacrificing one of the best of the flock. Imitating Jesus (Phil. 2:5-11) meant following in His voluntary suffering. Offering ourselves as "living sacrifices" (Rom. 12:1) implies personal cost of some sort.

(3) Solidarity: taking action to identify ourselves with those in need. The writer of Hebrews sums it up this way: "Remember those in prison as if you were their fellow prisoners, and those who are mistreated as if you yourselves were suffering" (Heb. 13:3).

Perhaps the greatest call for solidarity is found in Isaiah 58. Through him, the Lord speaks to correct errant practices of fasting.

> Is not this the kind of fasting I have chosen:
> to loose the chains of injustice
> and untie the cords of the yoke?
> Is it not to share your food with the hungry
> and to provide the poor wanderer with shelter—when
> you see the naked, to clothe him? (Isa. 58:6-7)

He concludes with a promise:

> If you do away with the yoke of oppression . . .
> and if you spend yourselves in behalf of the hungry
> and satisfy the needs of the oppressed,
> then your light will rise in the darkness,
> and your night will become like the noonday. (Isa. 58:9-10)

Fasting to identify with the hungry and help them through our sacrifice is the spirit of solidarity. By voluntary choice we become like the hurting persons, assisting them out of our abundance to break out of the cycle of poverty, homelessness, or oppression that binds them.

In light of what we know—both about our characters as servants of Christ and about the needs of the poor and disenfranchised in our world—we must respond. Jesus calls us to make changes in our lifestyles that reflect our perspectives as stewards investing in eternity, make intentional sacrifice in an effort to follow Him, and identify in solidarity with those less fortunate than ourselves.

The biblical bottom line: Jesus calls us to respond to what we know through simplifying our lifestyles.

The Greatest Affluence of All

As I walked through the streets of the Mamelodi Township outside of Pretoria, South Africa, I realized that these black people had been reduced to nonbeings by the apartheid system. They were politically and socially poor because another had taken away their choices.

In the squatter villages on the fringes of many Third World cities, the people arise early in the morning to try to survive another day. They do not ask, "What's for breakfast?" It is either another moldy crust of bread or nothing. They do not stand in front of the closet matching colors and wondering what to wear. They have only one outfit, and if they have two shoes, they are fortunate. Economic conditions have taken away their choices.

The ultimate plight of the poor is that they are without choices. They cannot determine their living areas, diet, wardrobe, or vocation. Unlike us in the affluent areas, they spend little time wondering, "What are my plans for the week or month?" Their goal is to survive the day.

As we enter into considerations about simplifying our lifestyles—ways that we can intentionally alter our living patterns so that we might live a more credible kingdom witness—let us pause to thank God for the greatest affluence of all: the affluence of choice.

For some reason, God has allowed us to be born into economic abundance so that we have choices to make about our lifestyles. We can choose to simplify. Even if we move into the gutters of Calcutta to live with that city's 1 million street

people, we still choose to do it. The essence of poverty is to
be without choices, and this is a poverty few of us will ever
experience. Thank God for the affluence of being able to
choose to simplify.

Getting Started

Earlier, we said that a world-class Christian lives a lifestyle
that is compatible. We try to live in such a way that reflects a
global perspective. In light of the awesome number of poor
and suffering in our world, we commit ourselves to traveling
light—so that we are freer to serve and less encumbered
with material concerns.

I wish the Bible offered a specific list of lifestyle requirements: how much money to live on, where to live, when to
begin a family, what kind of car to buy, etc. But it does not,
and therefore it is difficult for Christians to take a dogmatic
stand in answer to these questions. I prefer to focus on issues that call for unique responses before God in each church
and in each family.

PRINCIPLE: *Discernment.* We all do well to identify the cultural and economic pressures designed to make us more materialistic. "Aren't you hungry for a hamburger now?" The
advertisement cries to us from the television set about 9 P.M.,
just after dinner has settled. Our instincts respond, "Yes, I'm
hungry now!" And while we may not go out for a hamburger,
we may trek to the refrigerator because the TV just convinced us we were hungry.

The discerning ear identifies the lie. "No, I am in no way
hungry. I doubt if I know what it is to feel true hunger."
Discernment means recognizing the way that the advertising
media manipulates us:

● convincing us that we can make exorbitant expenditures
on vacations, face cream, or cars because we deserve it,

we're worth it, or we've earned it;

• stimulating us to buy things we're convinced we need when in reality the word *need* is a euphemism for our greed;

• making us feel that we are backward or out of step with the cutting edge if we do not own a car phone, vacation in Acapulco, or use the "Gold Card."

Even the church is not free from being sucked into the materialism of our age. Tom Sine writes, "The standard teaching in most evangelical churches is that you can have as much personal affluence as you want. . . as long as you don't have a materialistic hang-up. Wrong! It's more than an attitude problem. We live in an interconnected, interdependent world. And there is only so much to go around. If I use more than a fair share of the resources God has entrusted to me, someone else is going to go without."[2]

PRINCIPLE: *Chosen Hardship.* The issue of sacrifice arises here. If we aspire to live like Jesus, our lives should have an element of chosen hardship because we desire to grow in character and want to identify with those less fortunate than ourselves.

Chosen hardship follows the thinking of Ralph Winter, the great missiologist from the U.S. Center for World Mission. He advocates a "wartime, not a peacetime lifestyle" for Christians. Since we are engaged in spiritual warfare for the souls of people, Dr. Winter encourages everyone to cut back, even as every citizen made personal sacrifices during wartime in an effort to support the national cause.

If more Christians do not choose at least some hardship, the task of world evangelization will never be accomplished. Patrick Johnstone of WEC International writes, "This denial of self and a willingness to embrace all the implications of discipleship flies in the face of twentieth century North American culture. Unless we are willing for this, we will never get the job done. I fear many are using ways to try to evangelize that avoid the Cross."[3]

But what does "chosen hardship" mean to you and me? A young married Sunday School class came up with the following suggestions:

● choosing camping rather than a hotel on vacation (real camping—with tents, open fires, lanterns—not living in a Winnebago with all of the comforts of home) so that we can feel what it is to live that way;

● doing one ministry or service per month in obscurity: something that no one knows about except Jesus;

● consciously giving away something you know you do not need (or you know someone else needs more than you do);

● walking to work or taking public transportation to save money on gas;

● skipping one meal per week and saving the money to be sent to a relief agency;

● serving a holiday meal at a soup kitchen.

Elizabeth Brewster of Fuller School of World Missions articulated the lifestyle of chosen hardship for solidarity with the poor in the "Zaccheus Covenant" distributed at the Lausanne II conference in Manila (1989):

To implement the statements on the poor in the Lausanne Covenant and the Manila Manifesto, I covenant to:

● Fast and pray weekly or monthly, as a sign of my identification with the poor and my desire for their salvation and transformation (Isa. 58:5-8);

● Regularly review my possessions, purchasing, housing, transportation, recreation, professional equipment, and expenses in order to develop a simpler lifestyle (1 Tim. 6:6-8);

● Learn from the poor through visiting, worshiping

the Lord with them, working alongside them, and becoming friends with them (John 1:14);

• Speak up for the poor in defense of their rights,
even at risk to myself (Prov. 31:8-9);

• Continually encourage my church or mission agency to proclaim the Lord Jesus to the poor, to plant and
develop Christ's church among them, to give compas-
sionately, and to work for the removal of the causes of
their poverty (Luke 4:18);

• Annually review my commitment to this covenant
with a friend to whom I will make myself accountable
(Luke 19:8).

Signed _____ Date: _____

PRINCIPLE: *Don't Buy on Impulse.* One of the greatest haz-
ards of credit cards is the removal of economic limitation. "If
I can charge it, I can afford it." This caters to greed, careless-
ness, and a host of other bad motives that provoke us to buy
things on impulse. With credit cards, we do not need to plan,
budget, or think through our decisions.

Impulse buying leads to one of two negative outcomes. We
either end up living beyond our means (because we owe for
things that we purchased on impulse) or we find ourselves
owning things that we know we do not need (in the same way
we find extra junk food in our grocery bag when we go shopping before eating dinner).

One world-class Christian told me that his lifestyle choices
included "not wandering through the mall during my free
time." He told me, "When I go through the mall with credit
cards in my wallet, I am tempted to buy things just because
they look attractive. To wean myself from impulse buying, I
take a walk down the street, not through the mall."

PRINCIPLE: *Don't Buy If Sharing Is Possible.* Our society is built on a foundation of individual ownership, but responsible use of our resources should call some of this into question. For example, could families get together in a neighborhood and own one lawn mower since it is usually used no more than once a week per family? Do we all have to own our own freezers, or could households buy one large one and use it together? Can we save money by forming a neighborhood or church cooperative for buying food?

Since I write, people often ask me what type of computer I own. I do not own one. The church where I work allows me to use the word processor during off hours, so I can get by without owning. Sure it is a little inconvenient, but simplifying one's life will always seem an encumbrance to a society bent on personal comfort.

The ideas of sharing introduce us to other tough questions—Who services the mower? Who pays for the repair of the computer? How do we pay for the electricity used by the freezer? What if the buyer in the cooperative purchases food we don't want? The issue, however, is not ease; the issue is voluntary simplicity, and this may lead our churches to greater discovery of both working together in community and developing an attitude of openhandedness toward our possessions.

PRINCIPLE: *Beware of Debt.* Is it possible to stay out of debt in our world? When we read the biblical statements like "Let no debt remain outstanding, except the continuing debt to love one another" (Rom. 13:8) or "the borrower becomes the lender's slave" (Prov. 22:7, NASB), we surge with desire to stay out of debt, but then we start the process of buying a home or we get the tuition bill for college education. Debt-free? Tell me how!

Whether it is possible to stay totally debt free is not the issue for most people. The issue is the epidemic of debt that has swept our world. Just when we start to get all of our credit card debt paid off, some bank sends us a new VISA card in the mail with a $1,500 credit line. We spend beyond our means and then pay 18 percent interest or more to bail ourselves out.

A simpler life may mean destroying credit cards or, more realistically perhaps, determining to pay the monthly statement in full when it is first sent. With many families in the United States living at a lifestyle approaching 110–120 percent of their income, growing toward simplicity will take time and discipline. In the long run, it frees both the individual and the financial resources to stay clear of debt.

Every Christian and every church needs to do some hard thinking on this issue of debt. Some churches have determined not to build new buildings until all of the cash has been raised. Others pool their resources to help students go to college, especially those who are anticipating full-time Christian service.[4] The issue of stewardship arises again: What is the best way for me to manage the resources with which God has entrusted me?[5]

PRINCIPLE: *Beat the System.* My wife and I enjoy finding ways around the economic pressures of our world. Bargain hunting, using coupons, and looking for deals can help us acquire the things we need without being extravagant in expenditures.

When we were engaged, Christie started looking for a wedding gown. Several of our friends had spent in excess of $1,000 for theirs, but no matter how romantic we felt, we simply could not rationalize such an expenditure for the sake of a six-hour afternoon. We prayed about it, and she went bargain hunting. The end result? A beautiful gown in Filenes' Basement in Boston for $29.

During my seminary days, I needed a suit for leadership in Sunday worship, but I had no suit and little money to spend. Again, we prayed. Then we headed off to a "railroad salvage" warehouse to start shopping. For only $25 I got a Pierre Cardin suit that looked tailored to me and perfectly met my needs.

Beat the system. Used cars, discount outlets, buying in volume through cooperatives, and taking the time to research before purchasing can enhance our stewardship and cut back our spending. In the process, we can have fun.

Many Christians feel the greatest pressure of materialism around the Christmas holidays. Advertising makes us feel that our love for others is directly measured by how much we spend on them, and yet each year we ask ourselves, "Why did we spend so much this year?" Why not beat that system and get into creative giving at Christmas?

Alternative Gift Markets Inc.[6] offers an annual "My shopping list for the world" that includes presents for the homeless, sick, and needy—"unique gifts that build peace and understanding in our global village." Instead of buying multiple gifts for the person who needs none, consider these, given in the name of a person we love:

● $60 to pay for one year's tuition for a Palestinian child at the Presbyterian Al Amal Child Care Center on the West Bank.

● A gift to help feed a hungry person in the United States at one of many urban or rural food pantries: $5 per day.

● $1 for five pounds of seed to help people start farms in Ethiopia or Somalia.

● Blankets for use in refugee camps: $5 each.

● Pigs in Thailand ($4 per piglet, $40 per pig), ducks in Mozambique ($10 for a flock of ten), or trees in Haiti ($1 for ten tree seedlings) all offer options that keep us giving with purpose and beating the system.

PRINCIPLE: *Motives.* Addressing the issues of things, possessions, and "stuff" forces us to confront our motives. How owned are we—so owned by our things that we cannot share? How much value do we attach to our possessions? Do we equate our worth with owning? Tom Sine writes, "Whatever commands our time, energy, and resources, commands us."[7]

Scott Wesley Brown's song "Things" poignantly addresses us in our love of possessions. Read the words slowly:

Things upon the mantle
Things on every shelf
Things that others gave me
Things I gave myself
Things I've stored in boxes
That don't mean much anymore
Old magazines and memories
Behind the attic door,

Things on hooks and hangers
Things on ropes and rings
Things I guard that blind me to
The pettiness of things
Am I like the Rich Young Ruler
Ruled by all I own
If Jesus came and asked me
Could I leave them all alone?

Oh Lord, I look to heaven
Beyond the veil of time
To gain eternal insight
That nothing's really mine
And to only ask for daily bread
And all contentment brings
To find freedom as Your servant
In the midst of all these things

For discarded in the junkyards
Rusting in the rain
Lie things that took the finest years
Of lifetimes to obtain
And whistling through these tombstones
The hollow breezes sing
A song of dreams surrendered to
The tyranny of things.[8]

The World-Class Christian Spirit

Many people will arise today and enter terrible, horrible, no good, very bad days, but we can act to do something in response. We can choose to live more simply that others may simply live. There is enough to go around, but sharing our abundance with others will call us to cut back somewhere, to limit ourselves voluntarily, to live a lifestyle that reflects our knowledge of the condition of people in our world.

This is the world-class Christian spirit.

Chapter Eight

MONEY:
AT THE HEART
OF THE
MATTER

God loves a cheerful giver.
The Apostle Paul

Dr. Ken promotes a "health and wealth" Gospel that teaches God's design to make every obedient Christian wealthy. In his teaching, wealth becomes identical with God's blessing, and the love of money equal to the love of experiencing God's best.

Dr. Barry, on the other hand, teaches that money is the root of all evil (rather than the "love of money," which the Scriptures teach [1 Tim. 6:10]). He looks at the rich of our world and responds in pious disgust, "Well, they may be rich, but they are not happy." When asked why these rich people seem so happy, he says it is a result of their perverse minds. (I grew up in Christian churches where this attitude was taught, and as I grew, it was a troubling paradox to me to find that some of these incredibly affluent people were both happy and generous. While I agreed that money could not buy happiness, poverty did not seem to guarantee happiness either.)

We Christians fluctuate in a love/hate relationship with money. One group implies an approval of selfishness and greed, where givers make deals with God—giving $10 away in hopes of getting $100 in return from the slot machines of heaven. The other implies a disdain for money, making the handling of money, one of our most basic stewardships, into a necessary evil which is managed begrudgingly.

The biblical perspective of the world-class Christian lies between these two extremes. Dr. Ken teaches a partial truth; God does sometimes bless people with economic gain as a result of living by biblical standards. But it is not an absolute rule. If it were, the godliest people of the world would live in Beverly Hills or in Manhattan and the most unspiritual would live in abject poverty. Experience in the global church teaches us that this is far from true.

Dr. Barry, on the other hand, makes a legitimate biblical point: Money should never be taken lightly. Of the thirty-seven New Testament parables (many of which pertain to the kingdom of heaven), seventeen concern money, property, or stewardship. Managing our resources is certainly important to Jesus. The evil attached to greed cannot be dismissed as insignificant. Paul writes with intensity to Timothy: "People who want to get rich fall into temptation and a trap and into many foolish and harmful desires that plunge men into ruin and destruction. For the love of money is a root of all kinds of evil. Some people, eager for money, have wandered from the faith and pierced themselves with many griefs" (1 Tim. 6:9-10).

The toughest monetary issue facing us is that of stewardship. How can we manage the financial resources which God has put at our disposal? How can we stay balanced so that we neither venerate wealth as the sign of our obedience nor diminish it to a crude evil force?

Two truths characterize world-class Christian giving: (1) God calls us to be generous in our giving and (2) God calls us to be responsible in our giving. These two truths lead to two subsequent questions: (1) Why should we be generous? and (2) How can we give wisely?

Why Be Generous?

Generosity. Liberality. Openhandedness. Munificence. All these words should characterize the Christian who realizes the abundance which God has given us, especially in the affluent Western world. We have so much that we can choose to simplify and choose to be generous.

And yet, when the topic of money arises, the questions I get asked include, "Should I tithe (give 10 percent) *before or after* taxes?" "Do I need to give money away from the profits on my investments or can I limit it to just my salary?" "Can I include donations to nonprofit organizations which are not uniquely Christian to bring me up to 10 percent?" "Should I ever give a gift of money if it is not tax deductible?"

While these questions have some legitimacy, those who ask them have missed the biblical point of generosity. God calls us to be generous, and through generosity, we grow. If we spend our energy trying to figure out how to give the bare minimum and still be obedient Christians, we miss the freedom that accompanies generosity.

Generosity affects our attitudes. Remember Charles Dickens' Scrooge? When he lived as a miser, he was rich, alone, and grumpy. When he was transformed by his vision of the future, he overflowed with generosity, and his entire outlook on life changed. Suddenly his wealth became a tool for enriching the happiness of others, and when he did this, Scrooge's joy was multiplied many times over.

When we are transformed with our vision of the future (i.e., investing our lives now for eternity), we cannot help but be generous. Our perspectives change. We see that everything comes as a gift from God, and it is now our privilege to use our resources to enrich the lives of others.

Generosity increases our joy because it frees us. It releases us from the grip of money because we have courage to give it away. In days of economic uncertainty, many spend precious emotional energy worrying about the future. They fear either not getting what they want or losing what they have. Generosity puts our lives in a wider arena. We take our eyes off ourselves and realize that God is our provider, and He will take care of us.

Bernie grew up in poverty, and through the diligence of his father and his siblings his extended family became quite wealthy. In the process, Bernie became a Christian, and one of the first areas that the Lord touched in his life was money. To help Bernie from becoming possessive or greedy, God taught him generosity.

Bernie is very wealthy, but he is free from it. He lives with an openhanded generosity, giving away in excess of 50 percent of his income. He gives liberally of both money and time, serving people at his church and around the world. He took early retirement so that he could be free to serve. Bernie provides a sharp contrast with his siblings who criticize their brother. They hoard their money and remain tightfisted, fearing that they might lose it and return to the poverty of their childhood.

Generosity affects our perspectives of ourselves in the world. As Christ's ambassadors, we always look for ways to make our loyalty to Him known. Giving should never be used as some sort of pharisaic self-aggrandizement, but it does set us apart from the world in which we live. Our monetary habits make it clear that we are walking out of step with the values of our world.

C.S. Lewis articulated our distinctiveness from the rest of society in *Mere Christianity:*

Charity—giving to the poor—is an essential part of Christian morality: in the frightening parable of the sheep and the goats, it seems to be the point on which everything else turns.

He continues by describing how such charity ought to set us apart from our neighbors:

> I am afraid the only safe rule [about how much to give] is to give more than we can spare. In other words, if our expenditure on comforts, luxuries, amusements, etc., is up to the standard common among those with the same income as our own, we are probably giving away too little. If our charities do not at all pinch or hamper us, I should say they are too small. There ought to be things we should like to do and cannot do because our charitable expenditures exclude them.[1]

Generous giving affects our perspectives of ourselves in the world. When others might buy without restraint, we find self-control because as Christians, we commit ourselves to generosity. Lewis points out that even if generosity is not noticeable to our neighbors, it will be known to us because it will "pinch us" and keep us from living up to the economic standard of those who earn the same amount we do.

"Keeping up with the neighbors" will not be possible if we see ourselves as followers of Christ and live this commitment out in our giving patterns.

Generosity affects our worship. Writing out the weekly or monthly check to the church or ministry we support is an act of worship because it teaches us that everything belongs to God, and we act as stewards. In our church services more emphasis should be placed on the giving of gifts as part of corporate worship. Too many Sunday worshipers view the offering plate as some sort of church membership dues or admission fee.

Haddon Robinson highlights giving as worship because it reflects before God our attitude and level of sacrifice. "I believe God honors many poor people who don't give a tenth,"

Robinson writes, "because what they do give is a sacrificial amount in relationship to what they earn. Similarly, for many wealthy people, giving a tenth is a way of robbing God. Their tithe becomes a tip."[2]

Giving addresses a fundamental aspect of our worship. We kneel, physically demonstrating our submission to God. We hear the Word of God preached, symbolic of our commitment to live under its authority. We give, demonstrating to ourselves and God the understanding that our resources belong to Him.

Art recently became a Christian, and part of his growth has been learning the joy of generosity. After hearing of a need in our church family, he wrote out a check to cover the expenses related to the need. He told me, "Giving gives me a unique sense of partnership with Jesus. Since I have become a Christian, my whole outlook on my money has changed. Now I see that God has entrusted money to me so that He can touch other peoples' lives through me. Every week, deciding how to give more is spiritually exhilarating."

Generosity affects our world. Art reflects the fact that God wants to transform our world and the needs around us through our generosity. As stewards of money, we have been given incredible opportunities to affect our world and the advance of the Gospel.

Chuck and Debbie, a young two-career couple, wanted to use their wealth for the kingdom of Christ. They had purchased a new car several years earlier and had now paid it off. They told me, "We don't want to buy any more new cars, but we would like to use our monthly car payments to support an overseas ministry."

Instead of spending the monthly payments on themselves, Chuck and Debbie took the amount they had been paying on their car and gave it to a ministry which supported national evangelists in Third World countries. Their monthly gift supports an evangelist and his family, and their generosity has enabled him to be free of monetary concerns so that he could plant three new churches in a predominantly Muslim country.

Individuals, families, and churches multiply their own joy of giving when they discover ways to use generous stewardship to affect the world.

How To Give Wisely

"Who can I trust?" The words came from a generous giver at our church. He had picked up the newspaper and read another tale of embezzlement and financial mismanagement in the religious world. He continued, "I want to give—and give generously—but how do I know that my money will get where I send it? How do I know what reports to believe? How can I be sure that I am not being duped by some dynamic personality?"

Giving makes us vulnerable. We could give money away and then find it was misused. That is one of the risks of giving. But there are some helpful steps we all can take to keep from making mistakes with the money we desire to invest in the work of Christ.

Step 1: Give through the local church. Our own fellowship, the place where we "belong," is the best place to start giving. The local church allows us to integrate our giving with our worship, and it provides a system of accountability by which we can monitor how the dollars we give are being used.

When I give to my local church, I support the ministry that edifies me each week. Some people call this "storehouse tithing," giving the first 10 percent to the local congregation to which they are committed. Giving to the local church allows me to see where our money is spent. If the pastor is driving a Mercedes, I will know it. If the church is avoiding missions and spending money only on itself, I will read about it in the Annual Report.

Giving to the local church also encourages my involvement in it. When it is my stewardship that is being expended, I pay more attention to the Missions Strategy of the church or the staff members the church employs. Involvement is one way to help manage the stewardship I give even further.

Tom Sine challenges every local church giver:

Local churches need to make an evaluation. I encourage them to do an audit of where their time and money goes. In the churches I work with, 80 percent of the time and money stays right in the building. Tom Skinner has said we tithe to ourselves—we put money back in buildings, programs, and facilities.

If we're serious about the Great Commission and the Great Commandment, we should set a goal of at least 50 percent of the time and money going to causes outside the church building.[3]

The church exists for the benefits of its nonmembers. When we give to the local church, we can help make sure such an outward focus persists.

Step 2: Give regularly. In teaching the Corinthians about giving, Paul wrote, "On the first day of every week, each of you should set aside a sum of money in keeping with his income" (1 Cor. 16:2). Paul clearly teaches them the discipline of consistent giving.

Some prefer to give monthly or quarterly, but the principle is still the same: Disciplined giving will do the most good to us (reinforcing the fact that our money belongs to God) and to the people or organizations we support (providing them with regular income).

Regular giving is in contrast to impulse giving. The reason solicitations for money fill our mail boxes is the propensity of Americans to give on impulse. A fund-raiser from Oxfam-

America told me that over 90 percent of American households give something to charitable causes, but many of these do so upon impulse. While this might achieve the budgetary goals of nonprofit organizations, it loses the impact on us because we give without forethought, discipline, or worship.

Step 3: Give strategically. Whether on the personal or local church level, we do best by giving according to a plan. None of us can afford to give something to everything, so we need (as individuals and as churches) to decide where we can make our most strategic impact.

One of my friends has prioritized the work of Bible translation with the Wycliffe Bible Translators. His strategy focuses on getting the Bible translated into languages that currently have no Bible. He implements his strategy by getting involved in the church Missions Committee and encouraging us to include Bible translation in our missions giving strategy. He also concentrates the money that he gives outside of the local church on the work of Wycliffe.

Some choose to focus giving on the urban poor in the United States. Others favor education. Support of Third World leaders attracts some, while others give to radio broadcasters like HCJB (Quito, Ecuador), Trans World Radio, or the Far East Broadcasting Company.

Every person and church gets tempted by the vastness of the world to spread their giving all over the world. Churches which boast of 300 missionaries in 100 countries may be too concerned with having multiple pins in the "Missionary Family" map. As a result, they spread their support too thin. Strategic giving means deciding where we would like to have a substantial impact rather than simply giving broadly.

Step 4: Get involved with giving. Giving should not be reduced to an impersonal exercise in exchanging checks for receipts. We need to get involved, when possible, with the people and ministries we support.

Getting involved means reading newsletters and supporting people in prayer as well as through monetary gifts. Getting involved might mean going on campus to see the Inter-
Varsity staff person we support "in action." It could mean
participating in a Habitat for Humanity building project to
which we give support. In some cases, it means a trip overseas to visit a missionary or a national Christian leader we
support. Such a visit might be costly, but it usually results in
tremendous financial response because we enjoy giving to
people and ministries whose work we have seen firsthand.

The strongest churches in the Association of Church Missions Committees network link giving and involvement.[4] One
church endeavors to get a missionary visitor in every church
member's home over a yearlong period. Another features
overseas exposure trips which give a personal introduction to
cross-cultural missions to about fifty church members each
year. A third does a pulpit and choir exchange once per year
with an inner-city partner church so that these churches
which give to each other's ministries know each other
personally.

Step 5: Give cautiously. Several years ago, my wife and I
began giving to ministries in South Africa. We started receiving more solicitations (because some organizations sell their
donor lists to each other), and one group caught our attention. A polished brochure boasted of incredible successes in
ministry at remarkably low costs. On impulse, I was ready to
write a check, but my wife exhorted a more careful look.

The closer we looked at the organization, the more questions arose: Why did the director own two homes? Why were
there three members of the president's family on a board
with seven members? Why were they supporting a man who
was in political trouble because of his pro-Apartheid views?

The questions led to a personal meeting with the president. When our inquiries met with defensiveness and hostil-

ity, our fears intensified. We decided not to be involved in giving to that ministry.

Whenever we look to give to a church or ministry, we ought to ask questions. Does the agency belong to ECFA— the Evangelical Council for Financial Accountability, a group dedicated to helping Christian organizations maintain financial integrity? If not, then we ought to be able to ask questions like:

- How are missionaries and programs financed?
- How much of the amount raised by individual missionaries is salary? (Where does the rest go?)
- Are contributions to the organization tax deductible?
- What national (overseeing) organizations does the agency belong to?
- Are the financial records audited each year?
- Who makes up the board, and how accountable is the President to the board?

Being cautious does not mean being suspicious. It simply means thinking of our giving as an investment and investigating the work of the agency as we would any bank or institution that manages our financial accounts.

World-Class Giving

Dr. Haddon Robinson tells a story of his early days in doing fund-raising for Denver Seminary, where he serves as president. He approached a businessman with a financial need of $20,000 for a new phone system. The businessman asked, "How much would you like me to give?" Robinson, not wanting to be presumptuous, asked, "Could you give $1,000?"

The businessman wrote out the check, and as he handed it over, he told Robinson, "You insulted me." The comment stunned Robinson, so the businessman continued: "You asked me for $1,000, but you needed $20,000. Either you felt that I wasn't able to give much money, in which case you underestimated where I am financially, or worse, you thought I had the money but wouldn't give you more, in which case you insulted my generosity."[5]

Haddon Robinson left that meeting vowing never to underestimate the power of God to work through His people to meet great financial needs. That businessman, a world-class giver, was waiting to respond to the challenge of generosity.

We might not have $20,000 in our checkbooks waiting to be given away, but we all have some resources over which we serve as stewards. Utilizing our money to the glory of God is essential to world-class Christian discipleship.

"Remember this: Whoever sows sparingly will also reap sparingly, and whoever sows generously will also reap generously. Each man should give what he has decided in his heart to give, not reluctantly or under compulsion, for God loves a cheerful giver" (2 Cor. 9:6-7).

Chapter Nine

REACHING THE WORLD THAT HAS COME TO US

The alien living with you must be treated as one of
your native-born. Love him as yourself.

Leviticus 19:34

The visit to the hospital in October commenced an ordeal that would last for eight months. My mother-in-law was admitted that night and began a series of surgeries, recuperations, setbacks, and rebounds which would continue to May.

For the family, the next months were times of waiting, praying, and hanging around the hospital. When the most difficult times were over, we were still coming to the hospital regularly, spending almost every free evening visiting with her.

During these months, I started to ask myself, "Here I am locked into a schedule that brings me to the hospital all the time. How can I build a world-class vision in this environment?"

The idea came to me as I overheard two hospital workers from Haiti speaking to each other in Creole: Why not initiate more conversations with other patients and hospital employees, especially those with foreign accents?

Over the next few months, I met many men and women from Haiti, several workers from El Salvador, one from Nicaragua, another from Israel. There was an emergency room doctor from Saudi Arabia, an anesthesiologist from Bombay, a medical school student from Gabon, and a nurse from Mozambique. We met others from England, Portugal, Colombia, Germany, and Japan. Even in the hallways of one Boston hospital, we grew in our understanding of the global village in which we live.

The experiences in that hospital reminded us that world-class Christian involvement does not start overseas. It starts by looking for and reaching out to the world that God has brought to us.

The Melting Pot Reality

What country has the second largest black population? How about the fourth largest Spanish-speaking nation in the world? What country has the second largest Polish city, the largest Jewish population, the second largest Puerto Rican city, the second largest Hispanic population center, and some of the largest Haitian, Cuban, Dominican, and Guatemalan cities in the world?

According to Jerry Appleby, in *Missions Have Come to America*, the answer to all of these questions is the United States.[1] Only Nigeria has a larger black population. The United States in the 1990s may overtake Argentina and become the third largest Spanish-speaking country. Chicago's Polish population is second only to Warsaw, and there are more Jews in New York City than in Tel Aviv. With over 1 million newcomers each year, the United States will have less than 30 percent of its population registered as "white Americans" in the 1990s.

The newest members of the melting pot come to us in three basic forms. *International students* from all over the world pass through U.S. Customs each year to pursue undergraduate and graduate degrees. Many come from countries that do not allow traditional missionaries, and they come with stereotypes of the United States as a "Christian" country. Appleby describes international students this way:

> Temporarily uprooted from familiar social, economic, cultural, and religious surroundings, tens of thousands of international students are transplanted each year onto the soil of colleges and universities in the United States. The frontiers of foreign missions are no longer only in Tibet, Saudi Arabia, Mongolia, and China. They are also in Boston, New York, Chicago, and Los Angeles, for they have come to the United States in the presence of international visitors.[2]

Sadly, only a fraction of these international students get to visit an American home during their studies. As a result, they return to their countries either desperately lonely and bitter about their isolation while in America or disillusioned by the thought that dormitory life exemplified the lifestyle of "Christian" America. The leaders of International Students Inc.(ISI) estimate that as many as 70 percent of international students never get off campus into an American home. For this reason, the dream of Gordon Loux, president of ISI, is that "every international student will have one Christian friend."

The second large group of newcomers come as *immigrants*. Education, world travel, and international business has led many internationals to make the United States their home. In Boston, for example, there are over 50,000 Haitians, which is still less than half the size of "Little Haiti" in Miami (which is much smaller than "Little Havana").

In our little town of Lexington, I get my donuts from men and women from the Azores and Brazil. Large numbers of Indian and Chinese families move in regularly. After the end of the adult swim at the town pool, I was getting dressed as the children entered for their afternoon swim. Four boys came in together: one Caucasian, one Black, one Indian, and one Asian. In these four friends, I could see the international scope of the youth of our town.

And city life is even more diverse. The Southern Baptists have planted ethnic churches around Boston to reach out to Haitians, Hispanics, Cambodians, Laotians, Greeks, and Arabic-speaking people. A friend of mine pastors a church in New York City where fifteen different languages are spoken. Ray Bakke, urban specialist for the Lausanne Committee for World Evangelization, says that there are ninety languages spoken in his home city of Chicago.

Like international students, many of these immigrants come from countries where they have never heard the Gospel, and yet, when they come to the United States, they find themselves isolated and alone.

The third cluster of newcomers are the *refugees*. Some estimate this population as high as 1 million. These are the political or economic exiles who have come from the Middle East, Central America, and Southeast Asia—or anyplace where turmoil might drive them out.

Refugees represent a special call to the church of Jesus Christ because they are truly the "aliens and strangers" of our world. Homeless, displaced, and alone, these people will respond with unique openness to the love of Jesus demonstrated through His people.

Refugees often bring people into our midst who might otherwise never hear the Gospel. In the northwestern United States, a group of Laotian refugees come from a mountain tribe which is classified as a "hidden people group," and yet they have been displaced to a community where the Gospel is freely preached. Christians in that area can reach people who have eluded missions outreach for decades in their own country.

Reaching Internationals—Practical Ideas

Bill and Judy have become missionaries all over the Peoples Republic of China simply by opening their home to international business people who come to the area for six months of training. Nel has a friendship evangelism ministry that affects Saudi Arabia, one of the most Muslim countries in the world. Steve is reaching many from East Asia because he is willing to spend three hours every Saturday morning tutoring immigrants who desire to learn English. Chris helped a Christian graduate student from East Africa understand and respond to the secularistic viewpoints of his professors by inviting him to join a Bible study.

The ideas are unlimited for people with some creativity. Kathy Lay and her husband used unemployment as an outreach opportunity to internationals: "When my husband was laid off from work three years ago, he frequented a small donut shop near the unemployment office. Once a week for four months he talked with the Korean owner. Three years later we are still friends with him. We were the only Americans invited to his wedding, we prayed with him as his wife delivered their son, and we have spent time with them socially and in Bible Study."[3]

We do not need an enormous amount of creative genius; we only need to look around us, open our lives and our homes, and try to be friends.

Underlying all forms of outreach to internationals are at least three basic principles.

First, start on a *foundation of prayer*. Bill and Judy pray for the chance to meet people from the Peoples Republic of China in their community. Then they go and hang out at the Chinese vegetable section of their supermarket. One group of five seemed especially prepared by God. When Bill and Judy befriended them, they said, "We have two questions: First, can you help us use the public transportation? And second, we would like to go to a church; could you take us to church?"

Tom and Carolyn build on a similar foundation of prayer, and they open their house to international tenants. God has brought them Buddhist students from Malaysia, communist students from China, and Muslim students from Egypt. In each case, the students God has brought them have been very open to discussion about Jesus, and one became a Christian and is returning to his family and country with a desire to evangelize.

Don and Meg prayed for their Pakistani Muslim friend for years. She was warm to their friendship, but resistant to the Gospel, so they prayed. After six years of friendship, prayer, and occasional discussions about the person of Jesus, their friend put her faith in Christ.

Second, build on *friendship*. Friendship is the single most important ingredient in reaching out to internationals. They need friends who will help them grow comfortable with the confusing culture of the United States. One friend spent a morning orienting a family of refugees on how to use an American home—from electric stoves to flush toilets which were unlike anything they had ever seen before.

Reaching out to internationals does not require an unusual gift of evangelism; it demands only a willingness to be a friend. Many internationals come from family-oriented cultures, and they need us to invite them into our families. When Norm and Debbie invited his coworker from India over for pizza, they met his entire family. In the course of conversation, Norm and Debbie discovered that this man and his family had been in the United States for five years, and theirs was the first American home they had visited. Until that friendship started, the Indian family had depended on television to teach them about American family life!

Gordon Loux writes, "International students in the United

States are particularly vulnerable to loneliness and the disruption of a new culture. They need friends who can help them adjust to American life, answer practical questions, and ease the loneliness of separation from friends and family."[4]

Here are some practical suggestions on befriending internationals:

- Meet arriving students at the airport and make sure they have housing for the first few nights. The foreign student office on college campuses will work with us on this.
- Help them find permanent housing and get settled. Show them how to read classified ads.
- Take them on orientation visits to local stores and show them how to shop.
- Orient them to the laws and street signs. Provide them with city maps and bus schedules.
- Invite them home for meals or include them in other social activities.
- Sponsor or attend activities specifically for internationals. Churches sometimes try picnics, retreats, sporting events, sight-seeing tours, or trips to museums or zoos.
- Encourage those interested in learning about Christianity to attend church services or a church social event. Use the holidays of Thanksgiving, Christmas, and Easter to explain the Christian faith.
- Hold a one day conference at the church on Christian faith, using seminars on the Bible or Christian living — integrated with lots of hospitality — to introduce internationals to the basics of faith.[5]

Finally, *be a learner*. Learning about the country from which our international friends have come or greeting them in their native language expresses a deep interest in the people we are trying to befriend. If we want them to listen to us talk about Christianity, we reciprocate by listening to their views without condemnation or ridicule.

Joking about sacred cows with Hindus, laughing at fanatical Muslims, or demeaning the intensity of Roman Catholicism in Latin America or the Philippines is no way to show respect to our international friends. As people who believe in the value of every person, our lives should reflect respect for and a desire to understand our foreign friends.

Here again is another reason to be gathering information about our world. One international student from Cape Verde became my friend instantly simply because I knew where he lived and that he spoke Portuguese. A taxi driver in Atlanta almost drove off the road with excitement because I knew the names of three cities in his country of Nigeria. If internationals sense that we have a genuine interest in learning about their homes, they are usually very willing to share.

One final thought about learning: Some Americans grow impatient with internationals because they cannot understand the accents or the broken English. Learning implies patience. Ask international friends to speak slowly and do the same for them. (Remember to speak slower, not louder; internationals are not deaf, they are simply learning English.) The more internationals we befriend, the better we become at deciphering accents, pronunciations, and sentence structure.

The Impact

If we want to have an intense global impact in a relatively short period of time, investing in ministry to internationals is the best option. Ministering to international students usually means touching the lives of the future leaders of business, government, and education. Every time the King of Nepal or the Prime Minister of Pakistan is in the news, I lament that no one at our church took the time to try and befriend them when they were students here in the Boston area. If someone invested two or three hours a month in reaching out to them, the course of entire nations could have been changed.

Mark Rentz, a professor at Arizona State University, writes about this impact on national leaders through international student ministry:

Last year after we invited my foreign students to dinner, my wife and I were astonished to learn that we were in all likelihood breaking bread with future leaders. One of my students, Khaled, in replying to another student's question, mentioned that his father had been president for five years.

"Of what company?" I asked.

"Of my country," he replied.

His wife nodded, adding, "President Abdullah al-Sallal, Khaled's father, is commonly referred to as having given birth to North Yemen."[6]

A couple who now teach in Oman, a devoutly Muslim nation on the Saudi Arabian peninsula, told me that the Sultan of Oman is very favorable toward Christians in his country. He contributed land for the building of churches to accommodate foreign workers. The Sultan's unusual benevolence toward Christians stems from his experiences as a foreign student in England. When he studied there, a British Christian took him into his home and befriended him. That anonymous man's outreach now affects an entire Muslim nation.

Another result of outreach to internationals is evangelism with those who are not reachable through conventional missions. Christie, my wife, has an ongoing ministry to a lab technologist from India. She befriended him as she trained him in parasitology, and in the process, she touched a devout Hindu who had only misconceptions about Christianity up to this point.

A friend works with Chinese scholars who come to study at the Massachusetts Institute of Technology (MIT). One of the men who has come this year is from the Weega ethnic minority, one of the official "hidden people groups" listed by the U.S. Center for World Missions. If this man learns of Jesus this year, he may be God's agent for bringing the Gospel to an ethnic group which presently has no knowledge of Jesus Christ.

A businessman had a deep conviction about reaching Muslims for Christ, so he came to me about a job opportunity in Saudi Arabia. He hoped that such an assignment could put him as an evangelist near Islam's holiest city, Mecca. Further research, however, revealed that his job assignment would put him on an American compound with very little opportunity to meet Saudis. As he prayed about the opportunity, God led him to get involved in international student ministry in Boston, where there were many from Saudi Arabia whom he could befriend and evangelize freely.

A third impact of ministry with internationals relates to the training of cross-cultural workers who will go from the United States to other countries. The couple who now teach in Oman prepared by getting involved with Arabic speaking people here in Boston before they went. Now they are on their way, but as a result of ministry here in Boston, they speak Arabic fluently, and they have Arabic-speaking Christians in Boston praying for them in Oman.

When Tom and Victoria prepared for service in church-planting in Rio de Janeiro, Brazil, they went to the Brazilian Pentecostal Church about fifteen miles from their home. On their recent visit home, Tom thrilled that church by preaching in Portuguese about the work going on in Rio while they shared with him about their ministry in reaching out to the Brazilian community (more than 5,000) outside of Boston.

A couple preparing for service in Latin America attends a

Hispanic church. A team getting ready for service in Haiti
serves at a Haitian church in the city. A single man on his
way to serve in Taiwan becomes a member of the Chinese
Evangelical Church in town. The presence of internationals
helps train cross-cultural workers for the culture, language,
and traditions of the countries to which they go. This recipro-
cal ministry uniquely reflects the Lausanne Committee for
World Evangelization theme: "The whole church takes the
whole Gospel to the whole world."

The Best Story Yet

In his *Enabler* newsletter, Nate Mirza recounted the following story—perhaps the most amazing contemporary account
of God working through a Christian committed to befriending
an international who was all alone:

> In 1986, an Englishman, Graham Lacey, and some
> friends were in New York. They asked themselves who
> would be the loneliest man in New York City. Conclud-
> ing it was the Libyan ambassador, they invited him to
> Thanksgiving dinner. He surprised them by showing up
> and said, "If people knew who I am, they would spit in
> my face. Your country has just bombed mine. Your peo-
> ple don't like Colonel Moammar Gadhafi, my leader."
>
> After several weeks of interaction with him, Lacey
> received an invitation from Gadhafi to visit Libya in Au-
> gust 1987. During an audience with the leader in his
> Bedouin tent, Lacey was accused of believing a Zionist
> lie. He answered, "Sir, I know Jesus Christ personally.
> I've experienced Him in my life."
>
> After more than an hour's discussion, Lacey asked to
> pray with Gadhafi. Following discussion with his advis-
> ers, the Colonel looked him straight in the face and said,
> "Sir, you may pray."

"I prayed in the name of our Lord and Saviour," Lacey said, "for (Gadhafi's) salvation, for his wife's and his family's and for revival, for an unprecedented outpouring of the Holy Spirit's power in Libya."

Gadhafi embraced him and after more discussion with his advisers in Arabic, Lacey was told, "The distinguished leader would like you to pray again." As Lacey hesitated, Gadhafi told him, "Nobody has ever told me before about Jesus. Nobody but a Muslim has ever prayed with me. I would like you to get down on your knees and pray again. This time Libyan television will televise it."[7]

Chapter Ten

GOING GLOBAL

*To live life to the fullest, you have to
experience the world.*

Henry Stanley

The bumper sticker caught my eye: THINK GLOBALLY, ACT LOCALLY. The theme rings true for any who aspire to grow as a world-class Christian. God calls us to think (and pray and give and understand and live) with a global perspective and to act to affect lives right around us for the advancement of His kingdom.

But our local involvement also thrusts us outward. We desire to grow in our understanding of God's world, so we go beyond our normal comfort zones into involvement with other people from other cultures and (if possible) in other parts of the world.

Going global introduces us to risks. It is risky to try to relate to someone from a culture different from our own. It is risky to travel overseas to places where standards of hygiene are different than we might be accustomed to. It is a challenge to try to communicate with someone who does not speak our language.

Risk goes hand in hand with adventure. As we step out and take risks, we trust God in new ways which deepen our faith and makes our Christian commitment come to life. Paul Tournier, the great Swiss psychologist, writes:

> Throughout the history of the church, it has been this reversal in attitude [the desire for security and a risk-free environment] that has raised up martyrs and the heroes of the faith, has given them their indomitable strength, their complete independence as regards men and events, even at the times of greatest failure.... What matters is to listen to [God], to let ourselves be guided, to face up to the adventure to which He calls us, with all its risks. Life is an adventure directed by God.[1]

Low Risk Starters

Paratroopers do not start by jumping out of a plane; they start by jumping off platforms, getting used to the parachutes, and addressing their fears of height from the ground. Going global does not start with getting on a jet for the first time and leaving for the remotest jungles of Papua New Guinea, but it might start with correspondence with a worker from Wycliffe Bible Translators or New Tribes Mission in Papua New Guinea.

We can feel free to start small. Taking the risk of going out to eat international food might be all we can take. Eating "hot salsa sauce" at the Mexican restaurant might be a risk for us, but let's do it! Rationalizing that "Since I am not headed overseas, I need not have an interest in anyplace other than my home culture" misses the opportunity to learn in our ever-shrinking global village.

Larry Anzivino, the chairman of the missions committee at Grace Chapel, encourages these low risk starters for families desiring to build a world-class home environment:

- Host a missionary and let your family hear about life in a foreign culture. Help children see that people actually live in the countries they see on the map.

● Write to missionaries or foreign friends. (Author's note: of all of the influences that got me thinking about the world, the earliest I can remember was the impact of foreign coins and stamps on letters from international friends. Looking at these introduced me, as a child, to the fascinating reality that our "world" was not the only world.)

● Host an international student or a friend from another culture for dinner. Help the children know people of different cultures, skin color, and language.

● House an exchange student for a year; this truly internationalizes the family.

● Attend cultural events in ethnic neighborhoods to develop an appreciation for other traditions.

● Eat out together at an international restaurant once a month or several times per year.

● Keep a stack of prayer cards at the dinner table and pray for one missionary every time there is a family meal.

● Support an international project or a child overseas as a family.

● Take a vacation with a purpose (within the United States) to help at a missions headquarters or to serve by helping in a Vacation Bible School in an ethnic church.

● Make a phone call overseas to bring the work of our international friends into our world.

An article in *Moody Monthly* instructed readers on "How to Be a Foreign Missionary . . . Without Leaving Home."[2] Through prayer, correspondence, and a personal strategy, the author demonstrated how we can serve overseas by being partners with international workers there—even if we never go ourselves. When we start going global with even these small risks, it opens a new world of growth for us and our families.

Medium Range Risks

After we grow accustomed to the international outreach we can have from our home base, we can venture out a little farther. Now the risks and the investments take on greater commitments.

The Stevens family read prophetic words in an article by Tom Sine: "The United States and Western Europe of the nineties will continue to become more ethnically diverse. . . . Young people raised in the all-white suburbs of America and able to converse in only one language will become the culturally disadvantaged of the nineties. They will be ill-equipped to participate in the increasingly cross-cultural and transnational environment of tomorrow's world."[3]

Not wanting their children or themselves to be "culturally disadvantaged," Mr. and Mrs. Stevens enrolled in a Spanish course in a community college night school and encouraged their students to take Spanish in school. The family went on to commit themselves to serving in a Hispanic neighborhood in the city twice a year, and they try to worship at a Spanish-speaking congregation four times a year to help in their language fluency and broaden their understanding of the Christian church.

Language learning is time-consuming, humiliating, and sometimes frustrating, but it is a definite commitment to expand our cultural diversity in the internationalized world in which we live.

For the people at our church (a predominantly white, middle-class, suburban church), medium range risks include service ventures into the city. John Perkins, leader of the Harambee Christian Center in Los Angeles, exhorts Christians against the "Dangers of a Homogeneous Fellowship"; he encourages everyone to have Christian brothers and sisters from many racial and ethnic backgrounds. He observes that "Belonging to a group whose members are like oneself requires no faith. . . . Reconciling bigots is a far greater sign of the supernatural than is speaking in tongues."[4]

One of our young people, Margie Hanson, entered her first heterogeneous fellowship when she went to serve in the inner city. Her experiences were written up in *Campus Life* magazine as an example for other teenagers:

Margie's job in Newark (New Jersey) was to help in a day-care center with first- and second-graders. "When I first walked into the room and saw all these little black kids, I thought, I'll never be able to tell them apart"—a stereotype she didn't even know she held.

But within a day, she could not only tell them apart, she had fallen in love with them. . . . Margie went to Newark expecting to give, to help. Instead, she says, she was mostly on the receiving end, and she learned a lot about giving. Margie and the five others on the trip lived with several single mothers in government housing. . . . "They gave up their bedrooms for us. It was very hot that week and they gave us the only fan. They would get up early and make us an incredible breakfast every morning. They'd always wait up for us at night and do other little things, like put a Hershey kiss on our pillows."

Those two weeks in the inner city—two weeks in which she was the minority, the only white face in a sea of black faces—changed Margie. She realized that while she can walk away from the reality of interracial tensions after two weeks in the inner city—because she is white—many people can't. She determined to make a difference where she could."[5]

The experience of going cross-cultural in the city changed Margie's life and worldview. She went to college determined to work in the city, and at this writing, she serves at an orphanage in Calcutta, India.

Going global might not involve international travel. For Carol, it means a weekly trip to a homeless shelter to deliver meals that she and other homemakers have prepared. For Karl and Karen, it means leading a youth group of Cambodian refugees' children. For Ben, it means offering his painting services to inner-city ministries.

One other idea: Consider the handicapped. Although these people are usually not from a different culture in the usual sense, they do have a subculture of their own that needs to be penetrated with the love of Christ. And yet, the risks we take are real; we will feel awkward at first to work with the chronically ill, the hearing-impaired, the blind, or the mentally ill. But just as Margie Hanson grew through service in the inner city, we will place ourselves in a new environment where we are required to trust God when we serve the handicapped.

Medium-range risks take us into the world where people from other cultures and races actually live so that we might, in a small way, identify with them and their worlds. Following the example of Jesus (John 1:14), involvement sends us out to incarnate His love.

Higher and Wider Risks

A travel agency near Harvard University advertises travel with three words: "Please ... Go Away." In the world of Adoniram Judson, the first white missionary sent from the shores of North America, global travel for the average person was out of the question. It took him three months to sail from the East Coast of the United States to India. Today, however, we can travel from New York City to India in less than two days.

Edie Irish of Flint, Michigan illustrates the world of travel open to us. A member of the Traveler's Century Club (reserved for those who have visited 100 or more foreign countries), this 61-year-old grandmother has now set foot on 293 of the world's 308 nations and island groups. By making travel her priority, she has opened herself to all manner of exploration and risk, recently completing a trip to Libya and planning one to Angola and Chad.[6]

Traveling into other countries and experiencing other cultures is open to us as never before. With appropriate planning and saving, all of us can venture out to have our worldviews expanded by travel. The writers of *Travel and Leisure* observe that "Americans have come to look upon travel as a necessity—even a right—rather than as an extravagance."[7]

Bob expands his view of the missions world by extending his international business trips. His position has him overseas four times per year, and he uses free time and weekends to visit national churches, encourage international workers, and learn about the stresses of cross-cultural adaptation. His growth comes with a risk because it means leaving the security of Americanized compounds or conference centers and getting out on the streets of Hong Kong, Bogota, or Nairobi, but by making advance contact with missionaries or local believers, he is escorted by people who know the language and culture.

Hank is a single man who spends his leisure time on cross-cultural trips. He leads missions service teams or simply travels with some of the "adventure travel" groups in an effort to grow in his world vision. These vacations-with-a-purpose have resulted in Hank's service on the missions committee and increased financial commitments to international projects.

Short-term mission efforts that were once reserved for collegians are now available to adults of all ages. They give us the chance to visit the missionaries we support, see the work of the Gospel in another country, meet Christian sisters and brothers overseas, and grow in our understanding of the world. Consider some examples:

● My sixty-seven-year-old mother recently returned from her first-ever mission trip/vacation to a Third World country. She was willing to take the risk because a seventy-year-old friend challenged her to join in the expedition!

● Willow Creek Community Church, listed by *Christianity Today* as the largest church in America, prioritizes short-term missions trips because "we feel that one way to educate our people to God's worldwide program is through hands-on involvement. So short-term ministries into Mexico, even to the Inner City of Chicago and elsewhere, form a primary emphasis in our ministry."[8]

● Organizations like Wycliffe Associates or Hard Hats for Christ involve construction personnel in voluntary overseas service, especially at times of the year when business is slow back in the United States.

● Chris Eaton, director of Single Purpose Ministries, regularly challenges single adults to use discretionary time and income to serve in overseas opportunities.

Short-term service opportunities should not be some sort of affluent voyeurism, what one person critiqued as "Poor Tours." Instead, they offer involvement: "Get dusty. Stay for two nights with a Mexican family. Learn what the tourists never learn."[9] The higher risks of short-term mission travel are worth it because they offer growth and service opportunities that allow us to live alongside of brothers and sisters from every tribe and tongue and nation, giving us that "preview of heaven" referred to earlier.

Look For These Results
Going global is not merely an excuse for collecting experiences or accumulating new stamps in our passports. Our

reason for cross-cultural involvement is growth as world-class Christians. We go out so that we can grow as people whose lifestyles and obedience are increasingly compatible, in cooperation, and in accord with what God wants to do in our world through us.

When we start taking these low, medium, and high risks, we can look for *significant personal growth.* His travels across Africa in search of Dr. David Livingstone caused Henry Stanley to write, "To live life to the fullest, you have to experience the world." His experiences in other cultures widened his understanding of life itself. Even secular college organizations realize that personal growth comes from selfless service; a new program designed to use students' energy serving (and keeping them away from the raucous parties of Spring Break) advertises itself, "Instead of Beer, Volunteer."

On the Christian front, Chris Eaton writes, "Everybody says they go to serve and give, and every year they come back saying, 'I couldn't give enough compared to what the people gave me. What I learned far outweighs what I taught.' "[10] A student returned from a summer of cross-cultural service and wrote, "God taught me I was never alone. He was with me always. And every time that I was weak, He was strong. Every single time! He would always seem to turn my particular weakness into His strength, and that was amazing to see."[11]

On personal trips overseas or into other cultural settings in our own country, I have noticed that I pray more, consciously trust God more, and grow more. The heightened awareness of being out of control of my own life and trusting it to God makes my faith come to life in a new way.

When we go global, we can also look for *an enlarged perspective.* A recent injury on the basketball court led to surgery and three months in a cast. Although I struggled with the normal self-pity that accompanies any such inconvenience, I realized how overseas travel had changed my perspective. I could not complain. I had clean hospitals to go to and expert surgeons to consult with. A similar injury in a poorer, more remote part of our world might have left me crippled for life.

We do not go overseas or into new cultures to exert some sort of expertise we found through reading travel books. We go as servants and as learners. We go, asking God to change our perspectives, opening ourselves to the changes He wants to make in us based on what we see and experience. In training our summer short-term mission teams, we tell them that one of the purposes of our service is to help us understand that United States culture is not the standard by which all others are measured. We want them to be open to a change in perspective.

Dale Hanson Bourke, editor of *Today's Christian Woman*, wrote of her change in perspective that came as a result of a trip into another culture:

> I had just returned from a trip to Latin America, and the shock of reentry into American society was fresh. Everywhere I turned, I was amazed by our abundance of *things*. In the grocery superstore, for example, I stared at the produce department for several minutes, suppressing my desire to gather up the shiny red apples . . . and send them to the children I had seen begging on the streets of Guatemala City just a few days before. . . .
>
> I looked at the rack of reduced items and realized that the people I had seen living on the city dump would find the overripe fruit and dented cans to be unimaginable treasures.[12]

She goes on to describe her perspectives on contrasts. With the poor in the barrios of Latin America, she had seen a love of children and a wealth of sharing. With the rich in the United States superstore, she saw children abused and people living with dulled moral sensitivities. "I had seen wealth in spirit amidst poverty, and now I saw poverty disguised by wealth."[13]

When we go global, we can look for an *increase in our witness*. Those who spend their vacation time on medical caravans with the Christian Medical Society in Honduras get to share with their peers what they did. This sharing usually leads to an explanation of why they did it.

Friends who spend one weekend per month serving in the inner city often have great opportunities to share their faith with coworkers at Monday's coffee break when the discussion centers on "What did you do this weekend?" The outward expression of Christian faith through cross-cultural serving gives credibility to our commitment and people stand up and notice.

Christie and I have noticed that overseas service has given us the opportunity to share the Gospel with friends here at home who knew we were "religious" but never heard the Gospel. After our trips to places like Colombia or Nepal or Mozambique, they asked, "Why would you want to go there?" Our answers give us the chance to explain about what it means to be given over to the lordship of Jesus Christ.

Indiana Joneses for Jesus

The young boys in the Christian Service Brigade braced themselves for another boring speaker. It was "missions night," and some feared the worse. To their surprise, the speaker started, "How would you like to be an Indiana Jones for Jesus?"

The boys started to perk up, thinking, "Let's hear more about this."

"What is it that attracts us to the exploits of Indiana Jones?" he asked.

Boys started to raise their hands and fire out ideas:

"He lives a life of adventure."

"He goes to exotic places."

"He eats weird things."

"He hangs around with interesting people."

"He confronts evil powers."

"He seeks after and finds treasures."

"He lives on the edge of danger."

Then the speaker, a missions executive, described how the worldwide call of God needs young people who are willing to be Indiana Joneses for Jesus. He explained with stories about the need for men and women who would go out and take risks—even the risk of dying—to spread the Gospel. These adventurers for Jesus might go to places our world thinks are exotic—like Bombay, Kathmandu, Santiago, or Moscow—to tell people there about the Lord. Strange foods, fascinating people, exposure to the powers of Satan, and guaranteed danger lie ahead for those who followed God's call into other cultures. But, like Indiana Jones, they would persevere because they were after the greatest treasure of all: the treasure of seeing others come to know Jesus Christ.

The boys generally agreed that the missions speaker "wasn't as boring as we'd expected," and they went home dreaming of the risks that Jesus might call them to take.

If, as Tournier says, "life is an adventure directed by God," we face the challenge of being adventurers for Jesus. Will you step out and go global (even if it is only short-term) in an effort to understand and be more aware of our world? Taking such a risk will change your life.

Chapter Eleven

NEAR-SIGHTEDNESS

*The light that shines furthest shines the
brightest close to home.*

Oswald J. Smith

First Church has a tremendous global vision. A huge map in
the foyer highlights the missionary family in over 100 countries. A thermometer off to one side shows the progress on
the annual missions budget—each year the church has given
more to international missions than the year before—for the
past seventy years!

A visitor at First Church immediately notices the commitment to the worldwide advance of the Gospel, but after a few
months, discerning worshipers begin to notice the conspicu-
ous lack of concern for the local area. Millions of dollars are
raised for foreign endeavors, but there is little emphasis on
evangelizing the community.

One insightful staff member critiqued First Church this
way: "We are great on farsightedness, looking out for the
needs of 'the world,' but we are almost blind to nearsighted
issues. I fear sometimes that we excuse our personal responsibility to witness by highlighting our overseas involvement,
and, in so doing, we may help evangelize people half a world
away while our neighbors die without knowledge of Christ."

First Church's problems are not unique. Any church that takes on the challenge of producing world-class Christians can get so involved in the drastic needs of other places and cultures that we overlook the needs next door. Like the religious leaders of the Parable of the Good Samaritan, we run the risk of using our concern for world needs as an excuse for stepping over broken persons at our feet.

Oswald J. Smith, the pastor and missions-catalyst at the Peoples Church in Toronto, exhorted his people to stay balanced by observing that, "The light that shines the furthest shines the brightest close to home." He delighted himself in the global outreach of his church, but he knew that worldwide giving and missions conferences did not replace the need for outreach right in the community.

The world-class Christian grows by investigating, "God, what do You want me to do—starting right here at home?"

You Shall Be My Witnesses

A group at our church focused on training people for future assignments in other cultures. This "Potential Missionary Fellowship" met one week to study methods of cross-cultural evangelism, but as we gathered, I suddenly realized that I was not sure we could communicate the Gospel to our own people.

We deferred the lecture to the next meeting, and we spent the evening going over how to share Campus Crusade's "Four Spiritual Laws." I explained that this little booklet was not a perfect tool, but God could use it to help us get the message across.

Then came the assignment. Each of us was to share the "Four Spiritual Laws" (or some other Gospel presentation we knew) with one other person before the next meeting. One young man, who still had not grasped the need for "nearsighted" concern, raised his hand and asked, "But what if I do not meet anyone from another culture in that time?" I explained that he should look for friends, relatives, or co-workers with whom he had never directly discussed the Gospel. His outreach in these cases did not need to be cross-cultural.

Two weeks later, we met again. We started by sharing what had happened. Some had been totally unsuccessful; no one would talk with them about the Gospel. Others had gone through the booklet, but they talked about feeling awkward because it was the first time they had ever tried to explain the Gospel. The most dramatic story came from Fran. Almost two weeks had passed before she remembered the assignment, and she needed someone to talk to. The only person available was her aging father. Fran went through the "Four Spiritual Laws" with her dad, and at the close of the presentation, he prayed to commit himself to Jesus Christ! Fran was excited because she had never before talked with her father about knowing Jesus Christ personally and preparing for eternity.

Here was Fran, a potential missionary, preparing for overseas or cross-cultural service, witnessing to her father for the first time! The experience reminded me of Jesus' commission to be His witnesses in Jerusalem (Acts 1:8) first. Imagine what that meant for the disciples: to be witnesses in front of their friends, perhaps family, and countrymen; to speak boldly for Jesus before people who had seen them fail, deny Christ several weeks earlier, and then run into hiding.

We identify with those disciples because being a witness to the people we know is almost always more difficult. In some respects, for Fran to evangelize someone in a foreign land or in another culture—someone she might never again see again— might be easier than trying to be Jesus' witness to her father who has known her all of her life. The same might be true if we try to share the Gospel to any relative, longtime neighbor, or coworker who knows our sins and failures well.

A world-class Christian, however, is committed to outreach and evangelism at home or around the world. For many of us, the people we affect most are still those in our own culture and neighborhoods, so our commitment calls us to witness to them.

One of the motivations for witness is the spiritually lost condition of people who do not acknowledge Jesus Christ as Saviour (John 3:36). But we all must remember—as we study about "hidden people" who do not have any way of knowing Jesus or millions of Muslims, Hindus, and Buddhists without Christ—lostness is a spiritual state, not a geographic state.

In other words, my neighbor who worships financial success and my friends who live with no belief in eternity are just as lost as any person bowing down to a golden Buddha. A Buddhist in Thailand may appear more lost to me than my friend down the street, but from a biblical perspective, they both desperately need Jesus, and, at this point in my life, I can pray for the Buddhist, but I am in a position to present Christ to my neighbors and friends!

An interest in and commitment to world-class Christian outreach and evangelism begins right where we live. We cannot excuse witness in our community by an excessive interest in people beyond the reach of our personal evangelism.

Space does not allow for a detailed explanation of the "how tos" of witnessing, but there are some excellent resources available on this topic. The best include:

- *Life-Style Evangelism* by Joe Aldrich (Multnomah Press)
- *One to One Evangelism* by Leroy Eims (Victor Books)
- *Reaching Your World* by Beth Mainhood (NavPress)
- *Evangelism for Our Generation* by Jim Peterson (NavPress)
- *Out of the Saltshaker and Into the World* by Rebecca Manley Pippert (InterVarsity Press)

You Shall Be My Catalysts

Nearsightedness, paying attention to the needs right around us, obviously starts with an active outreach to those near us who do not know Jesus. But nearsightedness also means looking for ways to affect our churches with a world-class Christian vision.

Dick wanted to go into cross-cultural ministry, to a Muslim country in a tent-making capacity. We were catching up on the events of the past few months since he graduated college. I asked what I thought was a fair question: "Dick, if you desire to go overseas as one of our missionaries, why haven't you been involved in some aspect of our local church ministry?"

I expected comments about his being newly graduated or not knowing where to help or being too busy. I got something else.

"Well," Dick replied, his eyes widening as he got agitated, "This church—all churches that I know of—doesn't really care about the Great Commission. All I see are self-centered people, preoccupied with their own pet peeves (time of services, whether there is child care or not, and improving our physical plant), who have little interest in winning the world for Christ."

Dick's countenance changed from anger to shame. He had spoken his mind, but he realized that he was talking to the Minister of Missions, who represented both the "self-centered" people of the congregation and the funding that he needed to go out in service. I think he expected me to defend my case.

Instead, I simply replied, "Dick, some of your observations are true, although I think you have overlooked many fine people and churches. But this is exactly why I asked for your involvement. We need people like you to be catalysts toward greater missions involvement while you are here. You see,

Dick, whether we like to admit it or not, the local church is primary in God's worldwide purposes."

I then went on to point out four truths about the local church to him, truths that could help him change his perspective and become a catalyst for the growth of world-class Christians in our church.

Truth #1: *The local church is primary in world missions because Jesus said it is.* The promise of Jesus to Peter (Matt. 6:18) states that He will build His church and the gates of hell will not prevail against it. The image is of a forceful organization of believers representing one kingdom on the march against another. When the gates of that kingdom — hell — are attacked, they will fall.

Who is supposed to be on this attack? Jesus says it's His church. For each of us, this manifests itself in the local assembly of believers. The church fails in its task when it loses the mentality of advancement.

The local church that is a foe to world missions or a failure in doing its part in the Great Commission has usually degenerated from being a "kingdom-advancer" to a "fortress-builder." Rather than taking new ground for Christ, we spend our time protecting the turf we have.

Truth #2: *The local church is primary because the body of Christ is there.* Peer groups and campus fellowships can be wonderful stimuli toward discipleship and missions, but they do not present the whole cross section of the body of Christ. The local church offers the broadest range of spiritual gifts, a range that cannot usually be found in small group fellowships.

Truth #3: *The local church is primary because it affords us training and care.* I asked Dick, "Do you have the patience needed to persevere for years in a Muslim culture without seeing anyone become a Christian?" I answered for him, "No one really knows, but ministry to the junior highers at the local church can certainly help develop patience. And will you desire to lead people in another culture to Christ, disciple them, and encourage them to be world-class Christians? If you do, you have every opportunity to test skills, methods, and relational abilities right in your own church."

Truth #4: *The local church is primary because it is both the beginning and end of missions.* In his book, *A People for His Name*, Dr. Paul Beals identifies a three-part cycle in the book of Acts regarding the missions effort:

1. Evangelizing nonbelievers
2. Edifying the saints
3. Establishing churches.[1]

As soon as a church was established, the cycle resumed: evangelizing—edifying—establishing. The problem of the established church is that we perceive ourselves as being the end of the cycle, but not the beginning of a new one (the fortress mentality).

I concluded by asking Dick to come work with us as a catalyst to help make the local church into a gathering of world-class Christians.

How to Be a Catalyst

The intensity of a fire is measured not only by the heat it gives off, but also by the number of other nearby objects which it ignites. If we desire to affect our local churches with a global, world-class Christian vision, the place to start is with our own "fire." The best way to get others burning with a vision for prayer, lifestyle change, and outreach—both locally and worldwide—is to be on fire ourselves. As we grow in intensity, those around us will be ignited.

Beyond our personal example, however, there are some basic principles we can apply which will help us be a catalyst for a world-class vision in our local churches.[2]

PRINCIPLE: *Help make it manageable.* People come to

church for a variety of reasons. Some come to satisfy a genuine spiritual hunger. Others are coming to meet social, as well as spiritual, needs. Children and young people may come at the will of their parents. Hurting people come to be cared for.

The motivations vary widely, although spiritual growth is at least one of the driving forces. It is safe to assume, however, that most do not come to church to get overwhelmed by statistics, needs, and guilt-producing overviews of the task of worldwide outreach.

The realities of our world, however, are overwhelming:

● greater needs than ever with respect to health, hunger relief, and poverty;

● over 5 billion people now living on earth;

● urban sprawls that will soon (if they have not already) exceed the populations of some countries; if Mexico City reaches the anticipated population of 30 million by the year 2000, it will be more populous than Canada or Australia.

And these statistics just scratch the surface. The number of "children of the streets" in some cities, added to the people carrying the AIDS virus, plus the people in our own country who are responding to non-Christian religions that have come to the United States (like "New Age" Hinduism, the Black Muslim movement, or popularized "Zen" Buddhism) adds up to one word: OVERLOAD!

A zealous woman once attended our church, and she tried to instill a missions vision in others by quoting facts about needs and telling grim stories. She could quote so many statistics about world concerns that we nicknamed her "The Grim Heaper" because of her propensity to induce guilt.

For most people in our churches, the global perspective is too vast, too overwhelming. Therefore, painting pictures of millions or billions of people, thousands of "people groups," or hundreds of countries can be counterproductive in helping church members to see their participation in world evangelization.

World Vision once printed a poster that summed up the need for a manageable response. In the upper corner of the poster was a picture of a mass of suffering humanity. The question that followed: "How do you help 1 billion hungry people?" In the opposite, lower corner was a picture of one malnourished child. The caption: "One at a time."

One church has a large group of missionaries supported locally, in other parts of the United States, and in over twenty-five foreign countries. Even these facts overwhelm the average attender. Rather than encouraging everyone to get to know the missions family, the missions "catalysts" encourage people to adopt one missionary family. They give them "Prayer Packets" to help them start a relationship with one family. These packets include recent newsletters, a photo, a one-page summary of the missionary's work, and a self-addressed, stamped "air-o-gram" to get them started corresponding.

A recent attempt at one-at-a-time manageability in our church yielded a refrigerator magnet that said simply: "Do Something Once." The attached card gave people ideas of outreach that they could participate in just once: once a year (like going on the annual Walk for Hunger), once per month (write a letter to a missionary), once a week (witness to a neighbor), and once a day (pray for someone who does not know Jesus). The "Do Something Once" helps people move from the awesome world of 5 billion to our personal worlds of ones and twos.

Following are some other ideas to make missions meaningful, practical, and "one at a time" manageable:

● encouraging the adoption of one "people group" for prayer and research (the folks at the U.S. Center for

World Mission[3] are most helpful here);
• focusing on one missionary per month on a church bulletin board;
• asking the pastor to include one international prayer request per week in the pastoral prayer;
• recommending simple starter books on missions (see Resources listed at the back of this book).

Far better to start small and build, including the whole church, rather than overwhelming everyone and bearing the vision alone. The best catalytic action is to help people understand missions in such a way that they can make a personal, manageable response.

PRINCIPLE: *Present the global cause well.* The missions leaders requested and were granted space for a "Hall of Missions" outside of our sanctuary several years ago. We hung flags, put up some missions pictures, and assembled some racks for prayer letters. It was adequate, but not attractive.

We let the Hall of Missions stand until the day Bob approached me and said, "Paul, what are your plans for the Hall of Missions? It is a good concept, but it always looks like it needs to be dusted."

Bob is neither anti-missions nor narrowsighted. As a matter of fact, he is very supportive of international outreach. He was simply being honest. Our Hall of Missions looked shabby.

Many of us have had similar experiences with respect to presentations of missions. Some of them really "need to be dusted." Stereotypes of pith helmets, "missionary barrel" clothing, boring slide shows with out-of-focus slides (and the predictable sunset shot to close), and ill-prepared missionaries who really should not be preaching: These are the past images of missions that stick in some people's minds. Even if we are working to overcome the predictability, shabbiness, and poor performances of the past, we find ourselves swimming upstream in the local church in our efforts to present an international concern.

When battling the bad reputation of missions images, we can reverse the trend by trying to think of missions presentations in the light of the adage: "We never get a second chance at a first impression." If we do finally get the opportunity to present a global focus or an international report in a major church service, let's do it well. Has the Hall of Missions been dusted?

To help those who give international reports, we produce an informational bulletin entitled, "Doing Your Best at Grace Chapel." In it, we outline our church's constituency, our expectations of them as speakers, and our long-term plan for missions. We instruct our international visitors with advice like:

● We are very time conscious so please finish on time. We would rather have people leave saying, "I wish I could hear more" rather than "I thought he would never stop."

● "Man looks at the outward appearance, God looks at the heart" (1 Sam. 16:7). Both aspects of that verse are true. We desire that your clothing blend as much as possible with the church family. We do not want you to feel conspicuously under-dressed or over-dressed. As a result, we will do our best to instruct you as to attire that is appropriate for a given meeting. You will also be given a cash allowance for new clothes purchases to help you fit in best.

● Please be sensitive with your language during your presentations. Missionaries who talk only in terms of men can alienate our women. Also, referring to the national people as your "boys" is very offensive.

Sound harsh? Actually, our visitors are grateful for the help. As they make the cultural adjustment to the United States, they appreciate our efforts in making them culturally sensitive to us and our church.

PRINCIPLE: *Endurance.* Being a catalyst for a global vision in the local church is like swimming upstream. It is often easier to quit and resort to floating along with popular opinion.

Missions leaders, predicting the ability of the church to complete the Great Commission by the year 2000, list the local church as a major obstacle. Richard Sollis of New Tribes Mission states, "By insufficient vision, discipleship, and obedience, the church has bottlenecked the flow of personnel and resources needed to do the job."[4] Jim Reapsome of The Evangelical Missions Information Service, adds, "In a nutshell, apathetic Christians are the biggest hurdle to overcome."[5]

We need endurance in the face of apathy. Missiologist J. Herbert Kane writes in *Wanted: World Christians*, "After the second or third generation, Christianity tends to take on cultural overtones, and soon its members begin to take their heritage for granted and lose all desire to share their faith with friends and neighbors. The churches turn inward on themselves, and soon their chief preoccupation is their own survival, not the salvation of the world."[6]

We need endurance in the face of all that distracts our churches from an outward focus. A friend in ministry wrote to me, "We tried making missions a priority. We were going to learn about other countries, expand our missions budget, and add some missionaries to our support list, but we got waylaid by 'other things.' A few deaths in the church family, a church hassle over the Christmas program, and a staff resignation was all it took for our missions plans to be tabled for another year. I simply do not know how to make the 'over there' proposition of missions *real* to our people."

It is easy to give up. Genuine needs close to home deserve our attention, but we cannot let these needs diminish our overall commitment to see the Gospel communicated to all people. Farsightedness must be balanced with nearsightedness.

Endurance is the willingness to persevere even when there seems to be little support. Tom came to our church with a burden to see us involved with international students. At that time, only two or three families were interested. Tom persevered. Three years later, our church hosted the annual Thanksgiving Conference for International Students, Inc. Over 200 students attended, representing over forty countries. At that conference, almost seventy Grace Chapel families hosted students. Tom's endurance is bearing fruit.

Endurance in missions is the willingness to persevere even when there is little apparent interest. In 1978, we started sending young people out on summer mission service teams. At that time, only a few of our adults supported the idea. Now, over a dozen years later, the endurance has paid off: Over 400 young people, collegians, singles, and couples have gone out on over seventy service teams. The teams expanded in 1983 to include adults, and we have sent people as young as twelve and as old as sixty-nine into foreign cultures and needy areas in the United States. Summer missions service teams have been our greatest asset for building missions excitement and commitment at the grassroots level.

Brightening Our Corner

One of the Sunday School choruses of my childhood encouraged every Christian to "brighten the corner where you are." The idea in the song was that if every Christian would brighten his or her respective corner, more people could be introduced to Jesus.

The song highlights the need for world-class Christian nearsightedness. Investigating our role in God's worldwide commission commences with a look right around us. Are there people we can touch with the love of Jesus? Is there a local church I can ignite with greater concern for outreach?

Concerns "over there" in international settings cannot be our solitary focus. If it is, we will cease to exercise the day-to-day love toward each other which identifies us as the community of Christ. A commitment to missions should not imply a lopsided or one-sided view of ministry, but rather the nearsighted/farsighted balance.

Jack brightens his corner and acts as a catalyst for others to do the same. He is committed to evangelism; as a layman, he leads our training program for evangelism (our adaptation of Evangelism Explosion). He is active as a Christian witness in his place of work, and he is solidly committed to world evangelization as well. He makes sure that his Sunday School class knows and prays for missionaries; he involves others by informing them about international outreach efforts. He uses his international business travel opportunities to learn more about God's work in other parts of the world. Jack has a growing "bi-focal" vision, keeping both a commitment to "near-sighted" outreach/influence and "far-sighted" impact on others.

Chapter Twelve

GOD CALLS
WORLDWIDE

Here am I. Send me.
The Prophet Isaiah

It is frustrating to be given a responsibility to fulfill, but no instruction about where to start.

Several years ago, a team of young men from our church went to Whitehorse in the Yukon Territories. They went to serve at the summer camp of a church and to help expand the camp facilities by building two new log cabins.

When they arrived, the host was very busy. He took some time out one morning to show them the supplies, the logs, and the foundations on which the cabins were to be built. He directed them to another cabin that had already been completed and said, "When you're done, yours should look just like this one." Then he left. No drawings. No foreman. No plans. All they had were the raw supplies and the work force, but they did not know where to begin.

The team floundered about for a day, but finally realized that they did not know what they were doing. They found the camp director and asked for some help. An experienced build er visited with them for two hours. He showed them the basics for building the log cabins, insulating the joints, and constructing the roofs. He gave them what they needed to get started.

We live in a world that needs us to live as world-class Christians. The church needs men and women who will open their eyes, hearts, and resources to pray for and serve our broken world. But many of us—who have the raw materials and energies—have no idea how to get started. We might desire to care for and be involved in our world, but we have no idea where to begin.

In our youth ministry, I try to encourage students to grow in their concern for the world. In one meeting, I was quoting statistics with vigor—hungry people in the world, Muslims in Indonesia, churches persecuted by oppressive governments. I moved on to some specific facts about Burkina Faso in West Africa, when suddenly one of the students blurted out, "But I don't care about Burkina Faso!"

I was shocked. How could he be so calloused? As we talked afterward, however, I realized that I was the one in error. He was simply expressing his own frustration with the data I presented. It wasn't that he did not care about Burkina Faso or the people there. He simply did not know how to care. He was saying, in effect, "But I cannot care about Burkina Faso. I don't know how to get started."

He knew what he was supposed to do, but he needed help investigating where God wanted him to dedicate his efforts.

Considering A Global Call?
As we grow in our knowledge of and commitment to the world, we must at some time come to ask the question, "What about me?" Being involved with international students, giving sacrificially from our income, and witnessing to our neighbors may not be enough for us. At some point in time, we need to step back and ask God, "Should I be considering Your call into another culture?"

Al and Marilyn were on there way to a comfortable retirement when they heard that Abraham was seventy-five years
old when God called him out as the prototypical missionary.
The speaker continued, "And if you are under age seventy-
five, do not think that God couldn't call you. His call into the
world is not only for high schoolers or collegians. We don't
stop asking about His call after age thirty. What about you?"

Al and Marilyn now serve Christ in Europe, using the
skills that they had accumulated through years of military and
business experience. They sensed God calling them to something new, and rather than settle for a *status quo* retirement,
they went. They illustrate that we should consider a global
call as God prompts our spirits to do so—no matter what our
age.

As we grow as world-class Christians, study the needs in
other parts of the world, and befriend people from other cultures, those who observe us may respond, "Well if you are so
into the global advance of Christianity, what are you doing
here in the United States?"

It is a good question. If we seek lifestyles that are credible
with our Christian brothers and sisters, we need to take time
to ask, "God, what about me? Am I where you want me long-
term? Should I consider overseas service?" A global call may
come for us simply as the logical outcome of our desire to
live as world-class Christians.

Shortly before his death, the Christian musician Keith
Green wrote a tract entitled, *Why YOU Should Go to the
Mission Field*. He exhorts the body of Christ to consider
worldwide service for a variety of reasons. His reason #3:
"You should go because so few Christians are obeying the
call, making the need [for international workers] even greater." He observes that Amway and Avon have fourteen times
more representatives in the United States alone than the
church of Jesus Christ has outside of the United States.

On a worldwide scale, he points out that 9 percent of the world speaks English while 94 percent of all ordained Christian preachers minister with those 9 percent who speak English. When he wrote that tract, there were an estimated 1 million full-time Christian workers in the United States, while one half of the world's population (Muslims, Hindus, and Chinese) had only 2,417.[1] For Green, the inequities of the world were reason alone to consider if God were calling us to another land, "for how shall they hear without a preacher?" (Rom. 10:14).

Dr. Thomas Wang, a wise and venerated preacher from Hong Kong, speaks enthusiastically about the AD2000 Movement. In God's sovereignty, hundreds of Christians all over the world have simultaneously been planning strategies to complete the task of world evangelization by the year 2000.

Organizations are cooperating as never before to bring the Good News about Jesus to all people. Echoing the cry of the Student Volunteer Movement in the late 1800s, Dr. Wang and a host of others are calling for "the evangelization of the world in this generation." If we listen to these leaders, we should consider God's global call because of the unique times in which we live.

But What's Available?

In spite of devout Christian parents and a strong personal commitment to Christ, Will had never considered cross-cultural service. When I asked him, he responded without defensiveness. He simply observed, "I cannot preach, translate the Bible, or do medical work, so it never entered my mind."

"What do you do?" I asked Will.

"I am a construction worker," he answered. "I like to work with my hands."

"Then there are many places in the world you might go to serve. Perhaps you cannot translate, but if you joined Wycliffe Associates, you could build homes for people who will translate. Without people like you, they will spend their time doing jobs they are not qualified for."

Many of us understand Will's perspective because it is ours. We think that we have nothing to offer that would be useful in another culture or in missions work. Before dismissing the possibility, however, consider these truths about opportunities in missions today.

1. There is a greater diversity of people needed in cross-cultural service than ever before. A city team from Latin America Mission needs a bookkeeper, a dental hygienist, a child psychologist, and a business manager. The Evangelical Alliance Mission (TEAM) recently listed their needs worldwide which included:

- a teacher for missionary kids in Venezuela;
- a computer programmer in Colombia;
- a biomedical technician in the United Arab Emirates;
- an X-ray technician in Pakistan;
- a maintenance worker in Aruba;
- a secretary in France;
- a librarian in Spain.

The diversity of needs around the world makes it possible for almost anyone to consider a cross-cultural assignment in missions. A woman with grown children told me that her only qualification was her experience as a mother. I introduced her to the need for dorm parents at any number of schools for the children of international workers. "If you become their surrogate mother while school is in session," I explained, "you will be a partner with their parents who may be serving with a tribe in some remote village."

The opportunities abound, and sometimes the nontraditional international worker has access to countries which do not allow conventional missionaries. One missions executive writes, "At several points around the world medical personnel maintain the only officially-permitted Christian witness. Agriculturists work with local people to develop more stable food supplies, creating a reservoir of goodwill. Educational specialists lecture in universities, teach technical skills, function as TESL (Teaching English as a Second Language) instructors, and staff schools that cannot employ enough local teachers."[2]

A single woman considers using her degree and experience in plant pathology to help in a reforestation project in West Africa. A lawyer goes to serve the cause of the poor in the inner city. A veterinarian dedicates herself to helping with animal health in an agrarian society in Asia. A camp administrator looks into assisting the director of a Christian camp in Brazil. A TV scriptwriter dedicates himself to Christian broadcasting in the Philippines.

The opportunities make it possible for many to consider an international service opportunity.

2. *Short-term service opportunities offer a chance to serve and discover if we should go into another culture long-term.* When William Carey went to India in the late 1700s, short-term missions were out of the question. It took months to travel to foreign lands by boat, and when these first missionaries went, they worked in pioneering mission settings with people who may have been seeing Westerners for the first time.

Although pioneering situations still exist today, the world has changed drastically since William Carey went out. Jet air travel, the existence of the Christian church in many parts of the world, and an ever-increasing awareness of other cultures makes short-term missions service possible. People now go across cultural barriers regularly for service opportunities that last two weeks to three years.

As a result of short-term service projects in Burkina Faso, Turkey, and Egypt, Kristin has entered college determined to prepare for international service. Her overseas experience confirmed her desire and ability to work cross-culturally.

Eric attended our church as an average, twenty-five-year-old bookkeeper until his two week service project in Venezuela. On that trip, he met missionaries who were just like him, and he saw opportunities to use his skills to assist ministries that were serving the poor. At this writing, Eric serves as a bookkeeper still—only now he manages the accounts of the Suakoko Leprosy Center in Liberia (West Africa).

Even Bob and Jean (whom I will refer to later) started with eight days of serving in West Germany. Then they decided to go on a summer of short-term service with Africa Inland Mission at their headquarters in Bristol, England. These two short-term experiences directed their steps and confirmed their call. Now they serve full-time in the international ministry of Campus Crusade for Christ.

Short-term ministries afford us opportunities to meet needs in other cultures while simultaneously determining if we should consider a long-term call.

3. *Tentmaking introduces possibilities for outreach into countries which are closed to full-time Christian workers.* Tetsunao Yamamori, president of Food For the Hungry and author of *God's New Envoys*, points out that 100,000 new envoys are needed to serve in countries closed to traditional missionaries.[3] These new envoys—"tentmakers" who, like Paul the Apostle, use their secular skill to provide for their income (Acts 18:3)—offer the only avenue for entrance into the countries where 90 percent of the world's unreached live.

Several years ago, Bart began to open himself to the Lord in a new way. He openly prayed with his wife, asking God to direct him on how he could use his banking training and leadership to further His kingdom. God led them toward North Africa, and, after training, he and his family departed for a Muslim, North African country which does not allow any Christian missionaries. He now works about twenty-five hours per week in a bank, enough to pay for their basic needs, and dedicates the rest of his time to befriending Muslims and sharing the love of Christ with them.

Jack and his family serve in Saudi Arabia, using his Ph.D. in molecular cell biology to enable him to teach at the university. Steve teaches English in China. Gene and Terry taught school to gain entrance to Nepal. Fred uses computer skills to serve in Malaysia. Many doors appear to be closing to conventional missionaries, but new doors are opening to those willing to use nontraditional means to gain entrance to these countries.

Mark Watney of the U.S. Center for World Mission writes, "The Missionary enterprise requires people from all professions. Nurses in a refugee camp in Pakistan, professors in a university in Shanghai, engineers in a consulting firm in Bahrain, or an English teacher in an adult school in East Los Angeles can all be tentmakers. Tentmakers are Christians who use their professions not for comfort and prestige, but to pry open unreached, poor, oppressed, and needy areas."[4]

4. *New horizons of worldwide opportunity are open to those who are willing to use their retirement years.* Al and Marilyn, to whom I have referred before, serve now in Europe. Through experience in the military, then in private business, Al and Marilyn lived in Asia, Latin America, and Europe. Al speaks five languages; Marilyn—"only three." They are exceptional people—no matter where they might serve—but they have chosen to give themselves to international work in their retirement years.

Al and Marilyn serve as "latter day missionaries" (a phrase Al coined). Using retirement income and good health, they have dedicated themselves to service internationally during the years many reserve for a leisure life in Florida.

Al and Marilyn do not serve alone. Bob and Jean (mentioned earlier) have retired early so that they could dedicate themselves to serve in the international ministry of Campus Crusade. Using their years of experience in personnel management, they serve the immense staff of Campus Crusade by helping to devise effective personnel policies.

Norm and Gladys use their retirement years to serve the staff of Jungle Aviation and Radio Service and Wycliffe Bible Translators. Using his computer experience and her nursing and administrative skills, they assist others around the world in the task of Bible translation.

Mission agencies find increasing numbers of retirees who desire to serve, and as a result, many older men and women, who are at least partly financially independent, are discovering greater purpose in their retirement years than they ever thought possible.

But How?

Determining the will of God concerning cross-cultural service frightens us. How do we hear God's voice? Will He make me do something I absolutely detest? How do I know?

There is no set formula for discovering God's will. Instead, consider this discovery like viewing a constellation. When we look into the night sky, we need to see clusters of stars to view a constellation. Only by looking at the overall group of stars will we see Orion or the Big Dipper. Focusing on one star does not give us the big picture.

In the same way, discerning God's will involves looking at the big picture. When all of the "stars" come into view, we begin to understand the big picture we call the personal will of God for us.

"Stars" that contribute to this big picture include:

• *Biblical guidance:* God will never ask us to do something contrary to His Word, but He demands obedience in the clearly revealed things, and obedience to the commission to make disciples may thrust us out.

● *Opinions of others, especially authorities over us:* If many people around us commend us on our cross-cultural sensitivity and encourage us to pursue international service, maybe God is speaking through them.

● *Gifts and abilities:* God has entrusted us with certain unique personal resources; how will we use them?

● *Opportunities and situations:* If our company asks us to serve overseas or our church leaders invite us on a short-term mission trip, God might be speaking to us.

● *Desires:* A veteran missionary once told me that a desire to travel might be God's way of directing me toward service.

● *Initiative:* Taking steps of faith in one direction can help us affirm God's will as He either redirects us or confirms the direction we take. The Student Volunteer Movement taught that we all should take steps toward cross-cultural service until God called us to stay home: "planning to go, but willing to stay."

● *Need:* While it is not the only star in the picture, it certainly shines brightly. God may use our knowledge of people without Jesus to compel us out. This certainly motivated Paul (Rom. 15:20; 1 Cor. 9:16-17) and many of the great leaders of missions history like Cam Townsend (Wycliffe).

● *Miraculous means:* Elisabeth Elliot, in *A Slow and Certain Light,* includes angels, dreams, audible and visible signs, and prophecies as ways that God guided in the Scriptures and possibly how He might guide us today.[5]

What constitutes a cross-cultural or international call? The stars in the constellation vary, but after we get a clear picture from God, He calls us to obey.

Getting Started

Is God calling us worldwide into some type of cross-cultural service? We know what needs to be done: Workers are needed all over the world. But how do we get started?

Three action steps, that we all can take, may help us find out where God might be calling us globally:

(1) *Start Small.* Malcolm Muggeridge writes, "Christianity is not a statistical view of life. That there should be more joy in heaven over one sinner who repents than over all the hosts of the just, is an anti-statistical proposition."[6] In other words, our little efforts do matter!

Todd and his friends decided that they could not respond to the more than 20 million people in Mexico City, but they went down to serve through Galo Vasquez, who ministers there, by offering collateral for a no-interest loan program designed to help break the cycle of poverty. Their efforts affect two or three families at the most.

Our small efforts do matter. We belong to the God of the "mustard seed," who takes the smallest of actions and makes them significant in His economy (see Mark 4:30-32). Tom Sine writes in *The Mustard Seed Conspiracy*, "God has chosen to change the world through the lowly, the unassuming, and the imperceptible."[7]

Start small to investigate how we might be used to serve someone else in our world.

(2) *Start Here.* Involvement with internationals, serving other cultures in our cities, or developing a second language skill can all take place without going overseas. Yet God can use these efforts to prepare us for something international.

Mr. and Mrs. Anderson decided to start building their world vision right at home. Each night they watch the network news together, but their growing world vision caused them to add a new response. They listen to the news, taking special note of the international reports. During the commercial breaks, they turn down the volume, and they pray together for the country or the issue that was cited. After praying about famine needs in North Africa, God led them there on an exploratory trip with World Vision.

Dick and Karen—aged fifty-seven—decided they should start right at home to explore the potential of serving overseas in their retirement years. They spent a year getting trained in personal evangelism and another year getting training in cross-cultural adaptation. They have no firm direction yet, but they are making themselves available to God anywhere by starting here at home.

(3) *Start Now.* "These are good ideas. I'll have to try them out some day when I have the time."

We will never find out where else God might have us if we procrastinate and never ask. If we are to grow in our vision of God, His world, and our part in it, we need to make it a priority. We need to start today.

The first action we can take is to submit ourselves daily to the lordship of Christ. If we realize that we belong to Him— "bought with a price" (1 Cor. 6:20)—we will desire to grow in our ability to see the world as He sees it. Our desire to understand and care for our world will arise out of our relationship with Christ.

Lou and Donna are starting now to ask if God wants them to serve in another culture. In spite of the pressures of being young parents, they tell others, "If we say, 'Our lives are too hectic to evaluate where God might be calling us internationally,' we'll develop a pattern of running from that question for the rest of our lives. Life will always be hectic, so we need to be opening ourselves to God's worldwide plans for us now— even if we think we're in no position to respond."

Dr. Ralph Winter, the brilliant missions leader at the U.S. Center for World Mission, stated, "Nothing that does not occur daily will ever dominate your life." If we do not start now to open ourselves to God as His living sacrifices (Rom. 12:1), we may never hear Him call us into an exciting opportunity to serve Him worldwide.

Start small. Start here. Start now.

Chapter Thirteen

YOU CAN BE A WORLD-CLASS CHRISTIAN!

No reserve. No retreat. No regrets.
William Borden

My wife and I have tried to apply the principle, "living more simply" to our purchase of cars. We never purchase a brand-new model, and we have preferred "seasoned," older models. In light of the costs of the car, the excise tax, and the insurance rates in our state, older cars have saved us considerable amounts of money.

One car we purchased, a pumpkin-orange Volvo, had over 100,000 miles on it. Nevertheless, it lasted for quite awhile (we retired it with 172,000 miles!). Its last winter, however, the mechanical problems intensified. The car would not start so we called the tow truck. After a few days in the shop, the mechanic told us, "I can get this baby started, but you'll never keep it going." We laid the car to rest in the junkyard.

When considering the incredible task of being world-class Christians, we feel like that old Volvo. "I can get my vision started. I can get excited about a few statistics, a good book, or an exciting speaker, but I'll never be able to keep my vision going. I'm already worn out, so sustaining world-class Christian growth is beyond me."

We might get started, but can we keep going? All of us get wide-eyed at the prospect of thinking of global issues, international outreach, or praying for world missions. We can barely make it through the winter or manage our household budget; how can we start caring about 1 billion people in China or the hungry in Latin America?

While none of us can fathom the vastness or the scope of world missions, we can start small and build our vision as part of our ongoing discipleship. In addition to increasing our appreciation for the awesomeness of the God we serve, a growing world vision will help us keep our personal problems in proper perspective.

Keeping Going Won't Be Easy

"Why do we get such great attendance at our Christmas pageants, but such dismal attendance at missions events?" The question stung. A concerned, internationally-aware Christian was simply observing the obvious. I gave a few trite answers in immediate response, but his question got me thinking.

Was it because our presentations were shabby? Perhaps, but we had been making concerted efforts to overcome this.

Was it because our speakers were boring? Maybe, but we had hosted some of the top missions speakers in the country, and the turnout at our meetings was still poor.

I finally realized that the focus of the two events was different. The Christmas pageant was musical, festive, and culturally acceptable. Although the Gospel message was present, it came in the form of a celebration related to a popular holiday.

In contrast, the essence of international, cross-cultural ministry is sacrifice. The Gospel is still present, but in the form of cross-bearing unselfishness and giving. The Christmas pageant could satisfy those that came to receive; world-focus meetings were for those ready to give.

The experience of evaluation forced me to realize that the challenge of being a world-class Christian is truly counter-cultural. Asking for unselfishness, sacrifice, and Christ-like service is foreign to a culture where our first question is often, "What's in this for me?"

Events that focus on international needs and cross-cultural service opportunities may never get the same type of attendance as concerts, Christmas pageants, or Easter services, but this may be because the world-class Christian challenge has not been understood.

Keeping The Vision Going

Managerial experts frequently use the saying, "Failing to plan is planning to fail." The saying holds true for our personal growth as world-class Christians. If we do not plan for expanding our vision through reading, prayer, experiences in serving, or simpler living, it probably will not happen.

To develop a growth plan, remember our definition of what it means to be a world-class Christian: *A world-class Christian is one whose lifestyle and obedience are compatible, in cooperation, and in accord with what God is doing and wants to do in our world.*

Keeping our vision going and growing means reading slowly over that definition and asking, "Where are my strengths? Where are my weak spots? Where do I need to start growing?"

Every one of us needs to grow in some aspect of that definition. Perhaps the best idea is to look over the following five areas and ask, "What goal could I set over the next year to assist my growth in these areas?"

Information. After one Sunday School class, a young man told me that he was going to commit himself that day to reading the international section of the newspaper. He said, "I usually read only the sports section, but I am growing to understand that God may want to use that newspaper as my guide for prayer today."

A world-class vision cannot grow without fueling the vision with information. Subscribing to *World Christian* magazine,[1] getting on a missionary's mailing list, or (if we are really zealous) getting the round-the-world "Pulse" report published by the Evangelical Missions Information Service[2] will help us get a better idea of some of the challenges facing the church worldwide.

Information growth might include learning geography (i.e., finding out the location of Guyana, Guinea-Bissau, Equatorial Guinea, or Papua New Guinea) or reading a biography of some great missionary.

Here are some sample goals that could be set by an individual or a study group for the next month, six months, or year. Informational growth is not limited to these suggestions; these are simply samples, but feel free to add your own:

- Buy an up-to-date map of the world or an atlas.
- Learn the countries of the world (or perhaps the countries of one specific continent).
- Do a study through the entire Bible to document God's commission to go into the whole world with the Gospel.
- Read *From Jerusalem to Irian Jaya* by Ruth Tucker (the documentation of Christian history through the collection of missionary biographies).
- Read one book on missions theology or one specific missionary biography.
- Attend an informational conference or seminar either on missions or on some issue in our world today.
- Do a personal research study on one country, culture, or issue of global concern (such as global warming, Communism, or the rich/poor gap).

- Buy a global-learning game (see Resource section) to help your household grow in geographic knowledge.
- Subscribe to *National Geographic* or some other source of international information.
- View a movie or video which will encourage our learning about some other part of the world.

The best fuel for world-class growth is information.

Intercession. Responding in prayer challenges our busy schedules because it takes time. It also challenges our faith because we may wrestle with our doubts about prayer's viability.

To build our vision in this area, it is important to look again to the psalmist and realize that praising God for being the Lord of the whole earth is our starting point. Worship reminds us of the Lord of the harvest, and all other needs that we bring before Him take on perspective under Him.

Many of the world needs are so vast that we feel compelled to respond in prayer, committing needs to God when we can make no other response. Patrick Johnstone's *Operation World* (STL Books) can help us learn about and pray for the world, or we may want to focus on the needs of one specific missionary. I start almost every meeting by thanking God for the freedom that we have to meet together as Christians; it's one small effort I can make to sensitize myself and others to those Christians who suffer for their faith in other parts of our world.

"What if I am struggling to pray faithfully for my family and friends? How can I add the world?"

We don't need to pray for the whole world, but we can expand our prayer horizons by adding one or two missions-related prayers to our daily intercession. We can pray with bifocal vision and grow.

Here are some suggested goals:

● Use *Operation World* each week to start a Sunday School class or a weekly Bible study. Read the entry of the day and ask one or two people to pray about it.

● Ask for a missionary's prayer letter.

● Do a study of biblical prayers, paying special attention to what they teach about the character, mercy, and outreach of God.

● Read Wesley Duewels *Touch the World Through Prayer* (Zondervan).

● Contact Overseas Missionary Fellowship for information on the regional prayer conferences they sponsor throughout the country (ask also for their brochure by Bill Wilson, "How To Pray For Your Missionary").

● Watch the news regularly (or read a weekly newsmagazine) and practice "arrow" prayers.

● Read the biographies of either Hudson Taylor or George Mueller to stimulate conviction about prayer.

● Start praying for one country or "people group" as you learn about it.

Paul exhorted the Thessalonians to "pray without ceasing" (1 Thes. 5:17, NASB). With a world before us, we will have plenty to "pray without ceasing" about.

Integration. Jeff and Judy are newlyweds; they are also committed to grow in their world-class vision. As a result, they have determined that integration of that vision with daily life means trying to avoid the trap of accumulating things. "When you are first married," they observe, "you think to yourself, 'Wow, our apartment is so empty; we need this and we need that.' We have watched our married friends, and it takes no time at all to get bogged down with 'stuff.' As a result, we try to keep away from unnecessary purchases. God may send us to some developing country to serve, and we figure that it is good experience for us to get accustomed to living with less."

If we do not incorporate our world missions learning into our daily lives, it will become mundane or irrelevant. We start integrating a world-class vision into our lives by listening to international reports on the news, reading about places we have never heard of in *National Geographic,* or putting a world map over our desks. (My wife and I have tried to integrate a reminder of the great world into which we are called by surrounding ourselves with world maps—place mats, a desk blotter, a pencil sharpener, a clock, a paperweight, and even a beach ball all set the world before us regularly!)

Below are some suggested goals to keep the vision of an integrated lifestyle growing:

- Do a Bible study on riches, stewardship, or management of resources.
- Read Tom Sine's *Mustard Seed Conspiracy, Why Settle for More and Miss the Best?* or *Wild Hope* (all published by Word).
- See if we can increase our financial giving 1/2 to 1 percent this month.
- Find an overseas project to which your Bible study or Sunday School class can give an annual gift.
- Label the coat hangers in your closet. The first time you wear the clothes, take the label off that hanger. After one year (or three to six months, whatever you determine), give away any of the clothes on hangers which still have labels. If we can go one year without wearing it, we can find someone who can use it more.
- Read Ronald Sider's *Rich Christians in an Age of Hunger* (InterVarsity Press).
- Next time you shop for clothes, buy something to be donated for use at a shelter for homeless people (Shelters have a crying need for underwear!).
- Give something away!

● Join with friends once per month or week to skip a meal and donate the costs to a relief agency.

● Challenge yourself to go for a week or month without saying "I'm hungry," "I feel starved," or "I need. . . ."

● Take a half day sometime over the next year to do a personal evaluation, asking questions like, "Where could I simplify my life?", "Am I being motivated by kingdom-of-God or materialistic values?", or "How can I develop greater thankfulness for all I have?"

Involvement. "Give me something to do." The speaker, a young activist from our college group, desperately wanted to put what he had learned into practice. He wanted to be a doer of the Word, not merely a hearer (James 1:22).

As our vision for God's world grows, we need to find ways to respond practically. Writing letters to encourage missionaries, setting aside time each year to get involved in a service project, or adopting an orphan from another country all serve to expand our sense of participation in God's diverse world.

Here are some practical goals to consider:

● Get some training on how to share the Gospel with friends and coworkers.

● Investigate the opportunities to reach out to immigrants or international students in the local community (or at nearby colleges).

● Take your Sunday School class or Bible Study group on a field trip into a new culture—this could mean an international meal together, a worship service with a church from a different ethnic background, or a partnership in serving some need in the community.

● Look into the possibility of an overseas short-term experience, perhaps serving with one of your church's supported mission families.

● Participate in a project at an inner-city ministry.

● Learn a few greetings in another language, preferably one spoken by people who live nearby.

● Start praying for and targeting ways to reach out to subgroups in the community that may usually be over-looked (the police, night shift workers, the medical community, etc.).

● Write a letter every month simply to encourage a missionary serving in another culture.

● Host a missionary in your home and invite friends to come meet him or her.

● Organize an international student dinner at your church over one of the holidays (when they may be in the dormitories and most lonely).

Don't just stand there; do something!

Investigation. At some point in time, as our vision grows, we will all have to wrestle with the questions: "What about me?" "Where do I fit?" "Where do I need to grow toward fulfilling God's design for me in this great world?" "Should I consider cross-cultural ministry?"

Opening ourselves to the lordship of Christ is basic to Christian growth. Perhaps He will call us into missions work, but He may direct us to stay right where we are. We will never know without opening ourselves totally to Him.

Some possible goals regarding investigation might include:

● Reading a book on discerning the will of God like *A Slow and Certain Light* by Elisabeth Elliot or *Decision-Making and the Will of God* by Garry Friesen (Multnomah).

● Experimenting with God's call by getting involved in a ministry and discovering if we have the gifts and abilities to match the requirements.

● Look for opportunities to be a world-minded catalyst in your church, perhaps by joining (or starting) the international missions committee or by helping to present the global challenge to others.

● Evaluate your retirement plans now; how could you use those golden years in some sort of cross-cultural service?

● Look into the needs for "tentmakers" to limited access countries. Could your profession help gain entry to a country where missionaries are not allowed?

● Ask others to help us discover our gifts and abilities.

● Mobilize others for world concerns by giving them manageable tasks for learning or growth.

● Commit our children or grandchildren to the Lord, even if that means their involvement in some international setting.

All of us have some part to play in God's worldwide plan, but it may take some serious investigation to discover exactly where He may want us in the days ahead.

Just Do It!

Growing as world-class Christians requires the discipline of exercise. In the same way that we combat the procrastination and excuses that keep us from jogging, biking, or swimming, we will need diligence to continue to grow with a world vision. The folks at Nike athletic shoes give us the exhortation we need; we know what needs to be done—JUST DO IT!

When I am prone to quit the task of trying to make world-class growth a priority in my own life, I remember people. I am motivated by the changes in people as they have opened their eyes to God's world and their hearts to God's service.

I remember . . .

. . . Bryan and Janet, who have opened themselves to full-time ministry in a "second career" phase of their lives because they have been surrounded by world-class Christian friends;

... Marion, who chose to go to Haiti to serve meals rather than enjoy the rocking chair of retirement;

... David, who is using his international business travel to encourage missionaries and national workers in the countries he visits;

... Debbie and Norm, who got started learning about India by inviting an Indian family over to their home for their first taste of pizza;

... Nathan, who, at age five, does not have a broad world vision, but he is learning to say "Africa" with excitement;

... Bob, who has worked out his own international vision by leading over fifteen service teams and by serving behind the scenes at our international student functions.

All of these people have enlarged their vision for the world by investigating how God wanted to use them to have a global impact on their local church. These—and dozens of others changed by a greater view of God and His world—encourage me to continue toward the goal of being a world-class Christian.

In the 1800s, A.T. Pierson saw the Christian opportunity in his world, "a combination of grand opportunity and great responsibility; chance of glorious success or awful failure." Gordon Aeschliman observes that even greater opportunities face us as we approach the year 2000:

Never before has the shadow of the church been cast so far into distant places. Every tribe created by the hand of God now lives within the reach of Christians, be it through commerce, education, medicine, government, or neighborhood guilds.

Our hour is unprecedented, our jungle is uncharted, our opportunities are unmatched. There is only one village left in our day, and it is called Planet Earth. To be a member of God's international family as humanity steps into the twenty-first century is perhaps the closest we'll get to heaven in the flesh.[3]

LET'S DO IT!

Looking outward—developing a bigger view of the world—is an essential part of our continued world-class growth. The following resources include organizations, books, games (marked with an *) which help keep us outwardly oriented.

Aeschliman, Gordon D. *Apartheid: Tragedy in Black and White.* Ventura, Calif.: Regal Books, 1986.

Association of Church Missions Committees, P.O. Box ACMC, Wheaton, IL 60189.

Bakke, Ray. *The Urban Christian.* Downers Grove, Ill.: InterVarsity Press, 1987.

Barrett, David B., and James Reapsome. *Seven Hundred Plans to Evangelize the World.* Birmingham, Ala.: New Hope, 1988.

Barrett, David B. *World-Class Cities and World Evangelization.* Birmingham, Ala.: New Hope, 1988.

Beals, Paul A. *A People for His Name.* Grand Rapids: Baker Book House, 1988.

Borthwick, Paul. *A Mind for Missions.* Colorado Springs: NavPress, 1987.

————— *Youth and Missions: Expanding Your Students' Worldview.* Wheaton, Ill.: Victor Books, 1988.

Bread for the World, 207 East 16th Street, New York, NY 10003.

Bryant, David. *In the Gap.* Downers Grove, Ill.: InterVarsity Press, 1979.

————— *With Concerts of Prayer.* Ventura, Calif.: Regal Books, 1984.

Campolo, Tony. *Ideas for Social Action.* Grand Rapids: Zondervan Publishing House/Youth Specialties, 1983.

————— *You Can Make a Difference!* Waco, Texas: Word, Inc., 1984.

Christenson, Evelyn. *What Happens When Women Pray.* Wheaton, Ill.: Victor Books, 1976.

Compassion International, P.O. Box 7000, Colorado Springs, CO 80933.

Douglas, J.D., ed. *Proclaim Christ Until He Comes*. Minneapolis: World Wide Publications, 1990.

Duewel, Wesley L. *Touch the World Through Prayer*. Grand Rapids: Zondervan Publishing House, 1986.

Elliot, Elisabeth. *A Chance to Die: The Life of Amy Carmichael*. Old Tappan, N.J.: Fleming H. Revell, 1987.

_____ *Shadow of the Almighty: The Life and Testament of Jim Elliot*. San Francisco: Harper and Row, Publishers, 1979.

Elliston, Edgar J., ed. *Christian Relief and Development*. Waco, Texas: Word, Inc., 1989.

Engstrom, Ted W., and Robert Larson. *Hunger in the Heart of God*. Ann Arbor: Vine Books, 1989.

Estes, Steve. *Called to Die*. Grand Rapids: Zondervan Publishing House, 1986.

Evangelical Missions Information Service, P.O. Box 794, Wheaton, IL 60189.

Everything Is Somewhere: The Geography Quiz Book. New York: Quill, 1986.*

Fenton, Horace L. *Myths About Missions*. Downers Grove, Ill.: InterVarsity Press, 1973.

Food for the Hungry, P.O. Box E, Scottsdale, AZ 85252.

Frontier Fellowship Prayer Guide. Published monthly by the U.S. Center for World Missions, 1605 East Elizabeth Street, Pasadena, CA 91104.

Fuller, Millard. *No More Shacks!* Waco, Texas: Word, Inc., 1986.

Global Pursuit, published by *National Geographic*, Washington, DC 20036.*

Great Commission Handbook, SMS Publications, 701 Main Street, Evanston, IL 60202.

Griffiths, Michael. *Give Up Your Small Ambitions*. Chicago: Moody Press, 1974.

Inter-Christo, 19303 Fremont Avenue North, Seattle, WA 98133.

InterVarsity Christian Fellowship, Box 7895, Madison, WI 53707.

Jansen, Frank K., ed. *Target Earth*. Kailua-Kona, Hawaii: Youth With a Mission, 1989.

Johnstone, Patrick. *Operation World*. Waynesboro, Ga.: STL Books, 1986.

Kane, J. Herbert. *Wanted: WORLD Christians!* Grand Rapids: Baker Book House, 1986.

Keeley, Robin, ed. *The Quiet Revolution*. Grand Rapids: Wm. B. Eerdmans Pub. Co., 1989.

The Kneeling Christian. Grand Rapids: Zondervan Publishing House, 1971.

Kyle, John, ed. *Urban Mission*. Downers Grove, Ill.: InterVarsity Press, 1988.

McClung, Floyd. *Living on the Devil's Doorstep*. Waco, Texas: Word, Inc., 1988.

McClung, Floyd, and Kalafi Moala. *Nine Worlds to Win*. Kailua-Kona, Hawaii: Youth With a Mission, 1988.

Nunez, Emilio A. *Liberation Theology*. Chicago: Moody Press, 1985.

National Geographic. Washington, DC 20036.

Olson, Bruce. *Bruchko*. Carol Stream, Ill.: Creation House, 1978.

Olson, C. Gordon. *What in the World Is God Doing?* Cedar Knolls, N.J.: Global Gospel Publishers, 1989.

Operation Mobilization, P.O. Box 2277, Peachtree City, GA 30269.

Operation Mobilization Prayer Cards. STL Books, P.O. Box 28, Waynesboro, GA 30830.

Petersen, Jim. *Evangelism as a Lifestyle*. Colorado Springs: NavPress, 1980.

Pollock, John. *Hudson Taylor and Maria*. Grand Rapids: Zondervan Publishing House, 1962.

Richardson, Don. *Eternity in Their Hearts*. Ventura, Calif.: Regal Books, 1981.

_____ *Lords of the Earth*. Ventura, Calif.: Regal Books, 1985.

Roseveare, Helen. *He Gave Us a Valley*. Downers Grove, Ill.: InterVarsity Press, 1976.

Seamands, John T. *Harvest of Humanity*. Wheaton, Ill.: Victor Books, 1988.

Sine, Tom. *Why Settle for More and Miss the Best?* Waco, Texas: Word, Inc., 1987.

Stepping Out: A Guide to Short-Term Missions. Monrovia, Calif.: Short-Term Advocates, 1987.

Take Off! Dedicated to helping players learn the countries and flags of the world. Available through Department PAK89, P.O. Box 3999, Portland, OR 97208.*

Taylor, Dr. and Mrs. Howard. *Hudson Taylor's Spiritual Secret.* Philadelphia: CIM, 1958.

Tucker, Ruth. *Daughters of the Great Commission.* Grand Rapids: Zondervan Publishing House, 1989.

————*From Jerusalem to Irian Jaya.* Grand Rapids: Zondervan Publishing House, 1983.

U.S. Center for World Mission, 1605 East Elizabeth Street, Pasadena, CA 91104.

Wang, Thomas, ed. *Countdown to AD2000.* Pasadena: AD 2000 Movement, 1989.

Watkins, Morris. *Seven Worlds to Win.* Fullerton, Calif.: R.C. Law, 1987.

What On Earth (catalog of T-shirts, trinkets, and souvenirs with a global theme), 25801 Richmond Road, Cleveland, OH 44146.

Winter, Ralph, and Steven C. Hawthorne, eds. *Perspectives on the World Christian Movement.* Pasadena, Calif.: William Carey Library, 1981.

World Christian (magazine), P.O. Box 40010, Pasadena, CA 91104.

World Relief Commission, Box WRC, Wheaton, IL 60189.

World Traveler, published by Mr. World Traveler Ltd., Box 550, Needham, MA 02194.*

World Vision, 919 West Huntington Drive, Monrovia, CA 91016.

Yamamori, Ted. *God's New Envoys.* Portland, Ore.: Multnomah Press, 1987.

Yohannen, K.P. *The Coming Revolution in World Missions.* Altamonte Springs, Fla.: Creation House, 1986.

Notes

Chapter One

1. Howard Foltz, Missions Link, vol. 1, no. 7 August 1989, 1.
2. Chapter Two will define the term "world-class" as it applies to Christians. It refers not to the ability to "compete" worldwide but rather to the qualities of faith that are compatible, in cooperation, and in accord with what God wants to do through His people in this world.
3. Tom Sine, "Will the Real Cultural Christian Please Stand Up?" *World Vision,* October/November, 1989, 21.
4. "Lord of the Universe, Hope of the World" is the theme of InterVarsity's Urbana 90 Convention.
5. The term "Great Commission" refers to the final mandate of Jesus (recorded in various forms in Matt. 28:18-20; Mark 16:15; Luke 24:47; John 20:21; and Acts 1:8); a generally accepted definition summarizes the mandate as "making disciples of all nations." When this Great Commission is accomplished, most scholars believe it will prepare us for the Second Coming of Jesus (Matt. 24:14).

Chapter Two

1. Gordon Aeschliman, "Dancing on the Shrinking Globe," World Christian, May 1990, 9.

Chapter Three

1. Oswald Chambers, *My Utmost for His Highest* (New York: Dodd, Mead and Company, 1935), 288.
2. See Exodus 22:21; Leviticus 19:33-34; Deuteronomy 10:17-19.
All of these verses in the Law teach that the people of Israel were to love the lowly, alien, and stranger because they had themselves been aliens in Egypt.
3. Quoted from the World Vision International Christmas card December, 1989.
4. At the close of each Gospel and in Acts 1, we have a varied form of Jesus' Great Commission: Matthew 28:18-20; Mark 16:15; Luke 24:47; John 20:21; and Acts 1:8.
5. Chambers, 265.
6. Ralph Winter and Steven Hawthorne, eds., *Perspectives on the World Christian Movement* (Pasadena: William Carey Library, 1981), 9.
7. Many of these stories are found in Ruth Tucker, *From Jerusalem to Irian Jaya* (Grand Rapids: Zondervan Publishing Co., 1983).
8. Sylvia M. Jacobs, ed., *Black Americans and the Missionary Movement in Africa* (Westport, Conn.: Greenwood Press, 1982), 51.
9. This exciting story is told in Floyd McClung, *Living on the Devil's Doorstep* (Waco, Texas: Word, Inc., 1988).

Chapter Four

1. Brian F. O'Connell, "Understanding Your World," *Discipleship Journal*, Issue 41, 1987, 18.
2. Louis Wigdor, "Taking Global Education Seriously," *The Common Wealth*, Fall 1989, 1–2.
3. Ibid., 2.
4. *Church Around the World* is published monthly by Tyndale House Publishers, P.O. Box 220, Wheaton, IL 60189.
5. Evangelical Missions Information Service, P.O. Box 794, Wheaton, IL 60189
6. Anagrams by Beatrice Bachrach Perri. Answers: (1) Lisbon; (2) Madrid; (3) Helsinki; (4) Paris; (5) Tirana; (6) Prague; (7) Belgrade; (8) Warsaw; (9) Bucharest; (10) Copenhagen; (11) Athens; (12) London.
7. Morris Watkins, *Seven Worlds to Win* (Fullerton, Calif.: R.C. Law, 1987), 9-183.
8. Floyd McClung and Kalafi Moala, *Nine Worlds to Win* (Kailua-Kona, Hawaii: Youth With a Mission, 1988), 51–92.
9. Scott Wesley Brown, "Look What God Is Doing" from the album *To the Ends of the Earth*, Word Records, 1988.

Chapter Five

1. Carl Lawrence, *The Church in China* (Minneapolis: Bethany House Publishers, 1985), 117.
2. Ibid.
3. Tom Wells, *A Vision for Missions* (Carlisle, Pa.: Banner of Truth, 1985), 138.
4. Jim Reapsome, "What's Holding Up World Evangelization? The Church Itself," *Evangelical Missions Quarterly* (April 1988): 117.
5. *Reader's Digest*, January 1986, 171.
6. Wesley L. Duewel, *Touch the World Through Prayer* (Grand Rapids: Zondervan Publishing House, 1986), 186–87.

Chapter Six

1. David Howard, *The Great Commission for Today* (Downers Grove, Ill.: InterVarsity Press, 1976), 98–102.
2. Some of these suggestions appeared in my article "Around the World On Your Knees," *Discipleship Journal*, Issue 48, 1988, 10.
3. From the brochure "How to Pray for Your Missionaries," published by Greater Europe Mission, Box 668, Wheaton, IL 60189.
4. "Prayer Tips: Praying for the Unreached," *Co-Laborer* newsletter (The Caleb Project, P.O. Box 40455, Pasadena, CA 91114), Fall, 1989.
5. Portions of this chapter appeared in my article "Sharpen Your Global Prayers," *World Vision*, August/September 1989, 10–11.

Chapter Seven

1. Judith Viorst, *Alexander and the Terrible, Horrible, No Good, Very Bad Day* (New York: MacMillan Publishing, 1972), n.p.
2. Tom Sine, "Right-Side-Up Values in an Upside-Down World: Whole-Life Discipleship in the 90's," *Discipleship Journal* Issue 55, 1990, 37.
3. Patrick Johnstone, "The Cost of Evangelizing the World," *Alliance Life*, 3 Jan. 1990, 7.
4. Ken Sidey, "Debts Pose Problems for Missions Candidates," *Christianity Today*,

Sept. 1989, 22, cited the increasing number of students who are ready for the mission field but are unable to go because of accumulated school debt; in extreme cases, married couples anticipating missions have together accumulated school loans in excess of $30,000.

5. Some helpful resources for effective money management include: Ron Blue, *Master Your Money* (Nashville: Thomas Nelson, Inc., Publishers, 1986); Larry Burkett, *Your Finances in Changing Times* (San Bernardino, Calif.: Here's Life Publishers, 1975); George and Marjean Fooshee, *You Can Beat the Money Squeeze* (Old Tappan, N.J.: Fleming H. Revell, 1980); Richard J. Stillman, *Guide to Personal Finance: A Lifetime Program of Money Management* (Englewood Cliffs, N.J.: Prentice Hall, 1979).

6. For information, write to Alternative Gift Markets, Inc., HCR 6682, Lucerne Valley, CA 92356.

7. Tom Sine, "Will the Real Cultural Christians Please Stand Up?" *World Vision*, Oct./Nov. 1989, 21.

8. Scott Wesley Brown, "Things," from the album *To the Ends of the Earth*, Word Records, 1988.

Chapter Eight

1. C.S. Lewis, *Mere Christianity* (New York: The MacMillan Co., 1958), 81-82.

2. Haddon Robinson, in *Mastering Contemporary Preaching* (Portland, Ore.: Multnomah Press, 1989), 105.

3. Tom Sine, "Shifting Stewardship Into the Future Tense," *NAE Action* (March-April, 1990), 11.

4. The Association of Church Missions Committees (P.O. Box ACMC, Wheaton, IL 60189) is an excellent network for churches that desire to increase either strategies of giving or methods of involvement.

5. Robinson, 110–111.

Chapter Nine

1. Jerry L. Appleby, *Missions Have Come to America* (Kansas City: Beacon Hill Press, 1986), 8–9.

2. Lawson Lau, *The World at Your Doorstep* (Downers Grove, Ill.: InterVarsity Press), 12–13.

3. Kath Lay, "International Outreach," *Today's Christian Woman*, September 1989, 85.

4. Gordon Loux, "Reach the World From Your Living Room," *World Vision*, Feb.-March, 1990, 11.

5. Adapted from a list by Joy Cordell, "How to Launch a Foreign Friendship," *World Vision*, Feb.-March, 1990, 11.

6. Mark Rentz, "Diplomats in Our Backyard," *Newsweek*, 16 February 1987, 10.

7. Nate Mirza quoted this from *The Baptist Standard*, 28 June 1989.

Chapter Ten

1. Paul Tournier, *The Adventure of Living* (New York: Harper and Row, Publishers 1963), 153.

2. Angee Walsh, "How to Be a Foreign Missionary . . . Without Leaving Home," *Moody Monthly*, Dec. 1988, 29–33.

3. Tom Sine, "Shifting Into the Future Tense," *Christianity Today*, 17 November 1989, 21.

4. John Perkins, "The Danger of a Homogeneous Fellowship," *World Christian*, May 1990, 18.

5. Diane Eble, "Making a Difference," *Campus Life*, May 1988, 42.

6. "Globe-Hopping Mama," *First*, December 1989, 5.

7. Coleman Lollar, "It's the 1990's: Where Are We Going?" *Travel & Leisure*, January 1990, 135.

8. Jerry Butler, "International Ministries," *Willow Creek*, Nov./Dec. 1989, 27.

9. "Where In the World!" *Paraclete* (U.S. Center for World Mission newsletter) issue 1, 11.

10. Chris Eaton, "Short-Term Missions for Single Adults: Why and How," *Single Adult Ministries Journal* (February, 1988): 3.

11. Quoted in Alice Poyner, *From the Campus to the World* (Downers Grove, Ill.: InterVarsity Press, 1983), 151.

12. Dale Hanson Bourke, "Better off in Guatemala," *Today's Christian Woman*, Jan./Feb. 1990, 72.

13. Ibid.

Chapter Eleven

1. Paul Beals, *A People for His Name* (Grand Rapids: Baker Book House, 1988), 9.

2. Some of the following material is adapted from my "Overcoming Missions Malaise," *Leadership* (Winter 1988), 88–94.

3. U.S. Center for World Mission (1605 East Elizabeth, Pasadena, CA 91104).

4. Jim Reapsome, "Great Commission Deadline," *Christianity Today*, 15 January 1988, 27.

5. Ibid.

6. J. Herbert Kane, *Wanted: WORLD Christians!* (Grand Rapids: Baker Book House, 1985), 105.

Chapter Twelve

1. Keith Green, *Why YOU Should Go to the Mission Field*, (Last Days Ministries, Box 40, Lindale, TX 75771, 1982), 1.

2. Donald K. Smith, "The Many Faces of Missions," *Impact*, February 1990, 13.

3. Tetsunao Yamamori, *God's New Envoys* (Portland, Ore.: Multnomah Press, 1988), 58.

4. Mark Watney, "Wanted: 100,000 New Envoys," *The Caleb Project Newsletter*, February 1990, 3.

5. Elisabeth Elliot, *A Slow and Certain Light* (Waco, Texas: Word, Inc., 1973).

6. Malcolm Muggeridge, *Something Beautiful for God* (New York: Harper and Row, Publishers, 1971), 81.

7. Tom Sine, *The Mustard Seed Conspiracy* (Waco, Texas: Word, Inc., 1978), 23.

Chapter Thirteen

1. *World Christian*, P.O. Box 40010, Pasadena, CA 91104.

2. Evangelical Missions Information Service, P.O. Box 794, Wheaton, IL 60189.

3. Gordon Aeschliman, "Dancing on the Shrinking Globe," *World Christian*, May 1990, 9.

Leader's Guide for group study of

HOW TO BE A WORLD-CLASS CHRISTIAN

Paul Borthwick

Leader's Guide prepared by
LIN JOHNSON

Six Reproducible Response Sheets are
included at the back of this section.

LITERATURE
P.O Box 1047
Waynesboro, GA 30830
ph (706) 554-5827

1 2 3 4 5 6 7 8 9 10 11 Printing/Year 99 95 94 93 92 91

INTRODUCTION

Welcome to a most practical and challenging study. Though many believers are genuinely concerned about missions, they lack a vision that extends to the whole world. Others are so overwhelmed by the magnitude of the world's problems that they cannot—or choose not to—deal with them. And most believers simply don't know how to develop a world vision. Paul Borthwick understands these problems and offers manageable steps all believers can take towards becoming world-class Christians.

Before planning your first session, skim the entire text and this leader's guide. Read the introductory pages in this guide for help in teaching. Then prepare each session with the big picture in mind.

You will notice that a number of songs have been suggested for use at the beginning or ending of sessions. You may not be able to find all of them, but do include as many as you can. When biblical truth is wedded to music, we remember it longer and often experience greater conviction.

This guide also recommends numerous resources for use in class, primarily to acquaint members with what is available. Look through this guide and the text for suggestions, then order materials which are not readily available. Be sure to obtain a copy of *Operation World* by Patrick Johnstone, and try to have extra copies to give or sell to group members. This daily guide for praying for the world is distributed by Multnomah Press and may be ordered through a Christian bookstore.

Be sure to allow enough time for the application activities in each session. Stress the importance of being doers of God's Word, not hearers only, by following up on assignments the week after you give them. Ask the members to also share their victories, defeats, and related prayer requests. Lead the way with your own participation.

As you practice what you teach, and challenge your group members to do the same, may God help you all to develop into world-class Christians who share His global burden and vision.

THE PLACE TO BEGIN

Before you start tearing through this Leader's Guide, stop for a couple of minutes and read pages 4–7. These pages will:
- Tell you what you'll need to know to prepare each lesson.
- Introduce you to different methods of teaching your group.
- Help you evaluate how you're doing as a group leader.

KNOW YOUR GROUP

Picture the individuals who make up your group. What do you know about them? What do you need to know to lead them effectively? Here are a few suggestions:
- Develop warm relationships—get to know group members by name. Find ways to help members get to know each other as well.
- Find out what your group members already know and what they would like to know.
- Be a good listener.
- Promote an attitude of acceptance and respect among group members.

GET READY TO LEAD

If you are a little unsure of yourself because you're leading a group of adults for the first time, then follow the LESSON PLAN outlines for each session.

Using the guided discovery learning approach, each chapter will contain at least three sections:
- *Launching the Lesson*—activities that begin focusing on group members' needs.
- *Discovering God's Principles*—creative ways to communicate Bible truth.
- *Applying the Truth*—application activities that relate Bible truth to everyday life.

Some sessions may contain additional, optional sections such as:
- *Building the Body*—icebreakers and activities to help group members build relationships.
- *Prayer Time*—suggestions for praying together as a group.

REMEMBER THE BASICS

Read the entire text and this Leader's Guide. Underline important passages in the text and make notes as ideas come to you. Note any activities in the guide that take advance planning or preparation.

Follow these steps in planning each session:
- Make a brief outline of your lesson plan.
- Formulate and *write down* all the discussion questions you intend to use.
- Note all activities and teaching methods you plan to implement.
- Gather all the materials you will need for the session.

Each session should focus on at least one, and often several, Bible truths that can be applied directly to the lives of your group members. Encourage group members to bring their Bibles to each session and use them. It's also a good idea to have several modern-speech translations on hand for the purpose of comparison.

USE A VARIETY OF TEACHING METHODS

Response Sheets

Several Response Sheets are provided for you in the removable center section of this guide. Response Sheets are designed to increase your teaching impact.

The Response Sheets in this guide will help you enliven your sessions and encourage group involvement. They are numbered consecutively (Response Sheet 1 — Response Sheet 6) and show with what sessions they should be used. The guide gives specific directions for when and how to use each Response Sheet in the lesson material.

Brainstorming

Announce the question or topic to be "stormed." Group members may make as many crazy suggestions as possible, not waiting to be called on. Don't allow anyone to criticize the suggestions. List suggestions on the chalkboard; when all are in, have the class evaluate and discuss the ideas. This method loosens up the group, involves nonparticipants, and produces new ideas.

Group Bible Study

Each person should have her or his Bible open. Ask questions that will help the group learn what the passage you are studying says. Encourage sharing of insights as the group discusses the interpretations of the passage and its application to current needs. Always summarize findings. This method makes group members think; it shows them how to study the Bible on their own and it increases participation and involvement.

Discovery Groups

Divide the group into small groups of three to six persons. Appoint a leader for each group or let groups select their own leaders. Assign a topic to each group. Several—or all—groups may discuss the same topic if necessary. Allow 5–8 minutes for discussion in the groups, then reconvene and get reports from group leaders. Jot findings on the board for discussion. Many persons are freer to express themselves in small groups, so this method provides maximum participation and interaction.

Role Play

Two (or more) class members, without advance notice or written scripts, act out a situation or relationship. Give them directions as to the kind of people they are to represent and the situation in which they find themselves. They speak extemporaneously. This method helps people "feel" situations, gives them opportunity to try different solutions, and creates interest at the beginning of class.

Skit

Have members read the parts of a brief script that highlights a point, provokes discussion, or presents information. Provides good variety.

Diads

Like *Discovery Groups*, except that there are only two people, sitting next to each other, in each "group." (If a person is left out in the pairing off, assign him to one of the twosomes.) This method makes it easy for bashful persons to participate.

Discussion

In discussion, members interact not only with the group leader but with one another. Usually discussion is started by the group leader's asking a question to which there is more than a single acceptable answer. A student will respond to a question, someone else may disagree with him, and a third person may have additional comments. The teacher is responsible for starting the discussion, keeping it "on track" by asking leading questions as necessary, and summarizing it after contributions cease. If a discussion gets out of hand and rambles, much of its value is lost.

Here are a few guidelines for leading discussion:

■ Maintain a relaxed, informal atmosphere.

- Don't call on people by name to take part unless you are sure they are willing to do so.
- Give a person lots of time to answer a question. If necessary, restate the question casually and informally.
- Acknowledge any contribution, regardless of its merit.
- Don't correct or embarrass a person who gives a wrong answer. Thank him or her; then ask, "What do the rest of you think?"
- If someone monopolizes the discussion, say, "On the next question, let's hear from someone who hasn't spoken yet."
- If someone goes off on a tangent, wait for him or her to draw a breath, then say, "Thanks for those interesting comments. Now let's get back to . . ." and mention the subject under consideration, or ask or restate a question that will bring the discussion back on target.
- If someone asks a question, allow others in the group to give their answers before you give yours.

EVALUATE YOUR EFFECTIVENESS

After each session, ask yourself the following questions:

_____ How well did each group member understand the lesson goals?

_____ How many group members actually took part in the lesson?

_____ Could I use other teaching methods to increase group member interest and participation?

_____ Did I nurture personal relationships with my group members?

_____ How well did I prepare the lesson?

_____ How did group members react to me as a group leader?

_____ What do I need to do to become a better group leader?

WHY BE A WORLD-CLASS CHRISTIAN?

TEXT, CHAPTER 1

Session Topic
There are major benefits to being a world-class Christian.

Session Goals
1. To identify ways that *world-class* is used.
2. To examine the experience of a world-class believer and the personal benefits of being one.
3. To ask God for direction in becoming world-class believers.

Materials Needed
✓ Bible
✓ *How to Be a World-Class Christian*
✓ Copies of Response Sheet 1 for small groups; pencils

Special Preparation
1. Try to distribute the texts to members prior to the first meeting and ask them to read chapter 1.
2. Skim through Acts 13–20 and the opening paragraphs all of Paul's epistles for a feel of his ministry as a world-class Christian. Read Acts 17:1-10 as background for the Bible study in this session. Note any points you want to stress.

LESSON PLAN

Building the Body   *(5–10 minutes)*

Ask members to recall experiences they have had with other cultures—for example, reading, watching a television show, taking a short-term missions trip, meeting someone from another culture, listening to or talking with a missionary.

If your group is large, divide members into smaller groups for sharing. Be sure to participate yourself.

Launching the Lesson   *(5–10 minutes)*

Say: **"World-class" is used to describe all kinds of products and services today. In what contexts or kinds of advertising have you heard this adjective?** After members have responded, say: **"World-class" not only applies to all of these things you've named, but it also should describe us as Christians.**

Discovering God's Principles   *(35–40 minutes)*

Discuss: **Peter Wagner has said, "Once you decide to ask Jesus Christ to take control of your life, involvement in world missions is no longer optional." Why is this so?**

Summarize the responses. Then say: **Being a world-class believer, or one interested and involved in worldwide missions, is an exciting adventure, as we'll find in this study.**

One of the greatest world-class Christians ever was the Apostle Paul. Even though he was Jewish and had once persecuted those who believed in Jesus the Messiah, he became a missionary to the Gentiles after his conversion. Let's look at one of his experiences with people of a different culture.

Divide members into groups of four or five, appoint a leader in each group, and give him or her a copy of Response Sheet 1 and a pencil. Instruct the groups to read 1 Thessalonians 1–2 and answer the questions. If your study time is short, you may want to divide the passage into sections (for example, 1:1-10; 2:1-12; 2:13-20) and assign one section to each group.

Reassemble the groups and call for leaders to share responses. Supplement their answers as needed with the information following these questions plus other insights you gathered from your expanded personal study.

How did Paul minister to the Thessalonians? He told them the Gospel with power, the Holy Spirit, and conviction in the face of opposition (1:5; 2:2). He lived a true believer's life among them (1:5). He shared his life, didn't just preach to them (2:8). He went as a tentmaker and was no financial burden to them (2:6, 9). He encouraged, comforted, and urged them to please God (2:11-12).

What were his attitudes toward them? Thankfulness (1:2);

pure motives (2:3, 5-6); pure life (2:10); gentleness (2:7); love (2:8); longing to see them after he had to leave (2:17-18).

What were the results of his ministry with them? They welcomed the message of salvation as God's word (1:6; 2:13). They became believers and imitated both Paul and Christ, suffering for their faith (1:6; 2:14). They became models to the believers around them (1:7). Their faith in God was known everywhere (1:8-10).

What benefits did Paul personally experience as a result of being a world-class Christian? He acted as a true disciple, making other disciples (1:4-10); developed a servant attitude and desire to help others (2:1-12); pleased God (2:4); experienced joy (2:19-20); gained a crown in heaven (2:19).

Supplement members' answers to these questions as needed with material from the text:

- *What are other benefits of being world-class Christians?*
- *Why are these benefits important?*
- *How can they motivate us to become more involved in missions around the world?*

If any members have visited a mission field or participated in a missions trip, ask them to tell briefly how their experiences affected their lives spiritually and in other ways.

Say: **Being a world-class Christian is not just for people like the Apostle Paul or those who have already participated in missions trips. God wants all believers to get involved.** Have two volunteers read Matthew 9:35-38 and 28:18-20 aloud.

Applying the Truth   *(5 minutes)*

Summarize: **God invites and commands us to become world-class Christians. The opportunities and benefits are great. But most of us probably don't know where to start. That's why, in the sessions to follow, the author of the text will expose us to many practical suggestions. But first we need to pray for the desire to join His worldwide program and insight into His will for us all.** Close with conversational prayer.

ASSIGNMENT

1. Ask members to try to define a world-class Christian, then to read chapter 2 of the text.
2. Urge them to pray daily about taking part in world missions.

WHAT IS A WORLD-CLASS CHRISTIAN?

TEXT, CHAPTER 2

Session Topic
A world-class Christian obeys God and cooperates with what He is doing in the world.

Session Goals
1. To define *world-class*.
2. To define a world-class Christian and examine several examples.
3. To identify specific ways to develop a world-class lifestyle.

Materials Needed
√ Bible
√ *How to Be a World-Class Christian*
√ Length of newsprint or butcher paper, tape
√ Poster board, markers
√ Copies of Response Sheets 2 and 3, pencils

Special Preparation
1. In the center of a length of newsprint or butcher paper, print "World-Class is . . ." Leave plenty of room for members to fill in their descriptions.
2. With a bold marker, print on a sheet of poster board the definition that the author gives for a world-class Christian in chapter 2 of the text under the heading "For the Follower of Jesus." After the session, save this poster board for use in session 13.
3. To supplement the definition of a world-class Christian which the author of the text uses, consider the following descriptions:

A world Christian accepts these truths: The universal father-
hood of God, the universal lordship of Christ, the cosmopoli-
tan composition of the church, the priority of world missions,
the universal scope of the Christian mission, and personal
responsibility for world missions (from J. Herbert Kane,
Wanted: World Christians, Baker Book House, 1986, pp.
138–47).

World Christians are day-to-day disciples for whom Christ's
global cause has become the integrating, overriding priority
for all that He is for them. Like disciples should, they actively
investigate all that their Master's Great Commission means.
Then they act on what they learn. World Christians are
Christians whose life directions have been solidly transformed by a world vision (David Bryant, *In the Gap,*
InterVarsity Press, 1979, p. 73).

LESSON PLAN

Launching the Lesson   *(5–8 minutes)*

Before the session, tape the butcher paper to a chalkboard or wall
(without damaging the wall) and place some markers nearby. As
members arrive, have them write their first impressions of *world-
class* on the sheet. Be sure everyone writes something.

Read the responses to the group. Then say: **We have a variety
of impressions about the meaning of "world-class." Today we
want to clarify its meaning in relation to Christians.**

Discovering God's Principles   *(35–40 minutes)*

Display the poster board with the author's definition of a world-
class disciple and read it aloud: **"A world-class Christian is one
whose lifestyle and Christian obedience is compatible, credible,
and cooperative with what God is doing and wants to do in our
world."** Ask members to explain and expand on this definition.
After several do so, say: **Let's look at this definition in action in
the lives of four New Testament individuals.**

Distribute pencils and copies of Response Sheet 2. Divide members into three study groups and appoint leaders. Assign groups
the sections "Jesus," "Ananias and Barnabas," and "Peter" plus
the accompanying Scriptures. Instruct groups to complete the

studies for their individual(s) on the response sheet.

When the groups are finished, reassemble and ask leaders to report. Others may take notes on the response sheet as they listen. Supplement with these summaries as needed:

Jesus (Note: While not known as a Christian, He is our model.)

Demonstration: Jesus not only taught and preached God's Word, but He also performed good works to demonstrate His message. He was known as one who "went around doing good" (NIV). He spent time with outcasts, such as tax collectors and prostitutes.

Obstacles: Jesus had to overcome the Jewish prejudice against Gentiles and outcasts. He did so by ignoring that mind-set and demonstrating God's love for all people.

Results: People were healed and helped. Many believed in Him as Messiah and were forgiven of their sins.

Ananias and Barnabas

Demonstration: Ananias and Barnabas both ministered to Saul (later called Paul), a Jewish religious leader who persecuted Christians cruelly. He was their number one enemy at the time.

Obstacles: Ananias and Barnabas had to overcome fears of persecution by Saul plus doubts about his conversion. However, Ananias obeyed God's order, and Barnabas befriended Saul.

Results: When Ananias obeyed God, Saul was filled with the Holy Spirit, received his sight, and preached Christ in the synagogues. When Barnabas befriended him, Saul was accepted by the other believers and continued to preach. Because of Saul's conversion and acceptance by believers like Ananias and Barnabas, the church enjoyed peace and grew in strength and numbers.

Peter

Demonstration: God taught Peter that Gentiles could be saved too. Peter was willing to spend time with Cornelius and his friends and relatives and tell them the good news of salvation by faith in Jesus Christ. God's worldwide vision became his.

Obstacles: Peter had to struggle with the law stating that Jews could not associate with or visit Gentiles. He overcame this barrier by obeying what God taught him through an object lesson.

Results: Cornelius and the people with him became believers and received the gift of the Holy Spirit.

Discuss: **How did obedience to God help these men overcome obstacles that could have narrowed their ministries?**

Refer to the definition of a world-class Christian again. Have members find and read James 2:15-26 and 1 John 3:17-18. Ask:

- *Why is our obedience to these passages important in becoming world-class disciples?*
- *Why are good works crucial to a world-class outlook?*

Applying the Truth   *(10–12 minutes)*

Summarize: **The text author concludes this study with the following observation: "In *The Grapes of Wrath*, John Steinbeck summarizes the lives of several people with these tragic words: 'When they died, it was as if they had never lived.' They made no impact, left no legacy, affected no lives." Surely, we don't want to leave that kind of memory when we pass on. So let's think of the kinds of obituaries we would like to have.**

Distribute copies of Response Sheet 3, and have members write obituaries they would like to have as world-class Christians. Then have them list several steps they can take to work towards being the kind of world-class disciples that impact the world. Instruct them to place a star next to the step they will take this week.

Close with all praying silently about their goals.

ASSIGNMENT

1. Encourage members to post their obituaries at home as reminders to follow through on the steps they listed.
2. Ask for three volunteers to each prepare one or two 5-minute reports on modern missionaries of their choice. Caution them about duplicating reports. Instruct your volunteers to summarize the type of ministry each missionary had and to whom, as well as what we can learn today from his or her life and ministry. Suggest resources from your church library or other available collections. *From Jerusalem to Irian Jaya* by Ruth A. Tucker (Zondervan, 1986) is an excellent resource.
3. Instruct them to read chapter 3 of the text.

Planning Ahead

An effective optional opening for session 7 requires a slide show or videotape. Begin now to work on one of these productions if you have access to the needed equipment. Or assign the activity to one of your members who has an interest. See session 7 for details.

THE SCRIPTURES AND THE SAINTS

TEXT, CHAPTER 3

Session Topic
A continuing commitment to growth as a world-class Christian is motivated by a knowledge of biblical and historical perspectives.

Session Goals
1. To identify factors that help us persevere in our endeavors.
2. To discover biblical and historical facts that can sustain our commitment to world-class faith.
3. To select and use one encouragement to grow as a world-class believer.

Materials Needed
√ Bible
√ *How to Be a World-Class Christian*
√ Bricks or stones
√ Masking tape, wax paper
√ Markers, pencils
√ Chalkboard and chalk
√ Copies of study questions from *Discovering God's Principles*

Special Preparation
1. Complete the Bible study on all seven biblical missionaries listed in *Discovering God's Principles*. Then decide how many of these people you will have time to study. Make six copies of the study questions found in *Discovering God's Principles*.
2. Before the session, copy the list of names and references in *Discovering God's Principles* on the chalkboard.
3. Call the members preparing reports on missionaries in order to

offer any assistance needed and to encourage preparation.
4. If possible, bring a brick for each member for the application
   activity (see *Applying the Truth*). If you cannot locate bricks, try
   to find large stones. If neither is available, cut bricks or stones
   from construction paper. Cut 12-inch lengths of masking tape
   and stick them on individual pieces of wax paper so that members can more easily write on the tape before sticking it on a
   brick or stone.

LESSON PLAN

Launching the Lesson   *(5 minutes)*

Ask: **What keeps you going for the "long haul"? For example,
what keeps you from giving up in the middle of a project at
work or at home or for the church?**

Summarize members' responses. Then say: **In order to persevere as world-class Christians, we need motivation. Today
we're going to focus on two "foundation stones" that should
keep us going for the long haul.**

Discovering God's Principles   *(30–40 minutes)*

Say to the group: **The first foundation stone is the Word of God,
which introduces us to numerous missionaries. Let's look at a
few of them now.** Divide members into three to six small groups
or pairs (depending on the amount of time you have) and appoint
leaders. Assign each group or pair one of the following people
(except Abraham) and the corresponding Scripture passage, all of
which you have written on the chalkboard beforehand.

- *Elisha* (2 Kings 5:1-19)
- *Esther* (Es. 3:7 – 4:17)
- *Daniel* (Dan. 6:4-28)
- *Jonah* (Jonah 1:1-17; 3:1 – 4:11)
- *Philip* (Acts 8:4-8, 26-40)
- *Paul* (Acts 16:11-40)
- *Abraham* (Gen. 12:1-4)

Distribute pencils and copies of these study questions:

- *To whom did God send this person? Why?*
- *How did God use this person?*
- *What do you learn about God from this event?*

■ *What do you learn about being a world-class believer from this person?*

Each small group or pair will answer these questions for the person it has been assigned. If some groups finish early, have them answer the same questions for Abraham. When all are finished, reassemble and call for reports from each group leader. Then work through the questions for Abraham together. Ask: **What did all or some of these people have in common?**

Say: **These people were predecessors in a long line of believers who shared God's vision for the whole world. This historical perspective is the second foundation stone that can help us sustain our commitment to grow as world-class Christians. Now we'll hear reports about several modern missionaries.** Call on the volunteers to report at this time.

Point out that, except for Jonah, the missionaries you studied and heard about today were successful in God's eyes because they built their world-class visions and commitments on facts, not emotions. We need to do the same. Review the facts listed near the end of chapter 3 under the heading "Emotion Will Not Keep Us."

Applying the Truth   *(10 minutes)*

Ask: **What do you learn from these biblical and recent missionaries that helps you grow as world-class believers?**

Distribute the bricks, masking tape, and markers. Instruct each member to write on the tape one fact that will encourage him or her for the long haul of growing in world-class commitment; members will then stick the tapes on their bricks or stones.

Ask several volunteers to close with prayer.

ASSIGNMENT

1. Suggest that members put their bricks or stones in visible places as reminders to keep growing.
2. Encourage everyone to at least begin Action Item 2 or 3 at the end of chapter 3 of the text during the week.
3. Ask everyone who gets the newspaper or *TV Guide* magazine to bring to the next session (1) the current issue of *TV Guide* and (2) the news sections from a paper which may be up to three days old.
4. Tell members to read chapter 4 of the text.

INFORMATION AND ISSUES

TEXT, CHAPTER 4

Session Topic

To grow as world-class Christians, we need to be informed about the world and the issues that challenge the spread of Christianity.

Session Goals

1. To evaluate our knowledge of the nations of the world.
2. To explore ways to increase our knowledge of the world and its important issues.
3. To implement a plan to increase our knowledge of one area of the world.

Materials Needed

√ Bible
√ *How to Be a World-Class Christian*
√ World map; newsprint or butcher paper
√ Masking tape
√ Inexpensive objects bearing maps of the world (i.e., mugs, small globes) to give as prizes (optional)
√ Information resources
√ Recent newspapers, TV guide for that week
√ Half sheets of paper, pencils, marker
√ Chalkboard and chalk

Special Preparation

1. Trace a simple map of the world onto blank newsprint or butcher paper. Select ten countries, including some from every continent (except Antarctica) and outline their borders with a heavy marker; number them 1 through 10. Members will try to identi-

fy these countries from their shapes and locations, so choose countries that will be challenging but not too obscure.

2. Gather a variety of information resources about missions, such as magazines, missionary biographies, missionary newsletters, and reports. Be sure to include a copy of *Operation World*. If possible, bring extra copies of it to sell or give to members. For other specific titles, see the resources list at the end of the text. Also contact your pastor, church librarian, or church missions committee for suggestions and copies to bring to the session.

3. The assignment you gave the group about the Action Items at the end of chapter 3 is for you too. At least begin the work so you can encourage the others.

LESSON PLAN

Launching the Lesson (*10 minutes*)

Ask if anyone who began the Action Items from the end of chapter 3 in the text has something to share with the group. Share something that you found or learned, then move on.

Distribute pencils and half sheets of paper. Instruct members to number their sheets 1 through 10. Tape the world map you drew to the chalkboard. Point to each country you outlined, starting with #1, and have members write down the name of that country. Give members enough time to study its shape and location, but do not linger.

Members will grade their own papers as you name the countries. Find out how many got all 10 correct. You may want to reward these people with objects which have world maps on them.

Say: **In order to grow as world-class Christians, we need to be familiar with the world itself. Knowing the names and locations of countries is one place to start, but it is only a beginning. Today we will focus on a number of ways to increase our knowledge of the world and what God is doing in it.**

Discovering God's Principles (*30–40 minutes*)

State that the starting place for enlarging our vision is catching God's vision for the world. Divide the members into three groups. Assign each group one of these Scripture passages and have the members summarize what the verses teach about God's vision.

- *Matthew 9:36-38.* (We are to view people with compassion. Many are ready to believe in God, but there are not enough workers to work the harvest. We should pray for more.)
- *Matthew 28:18-20.* (God has commanded us to make disciples of all nations. This command was given to all believers, not just a few. We do not have to do this task alone; we have His constant presence to help us.)
- *Acts 1:6-8.* (We have the power of the Holy Spirit to help us in the task of world evangelization. The pattern we are to follow is to begin in the locale where we are, move out to reach our country, then go to the whole world.

Discuss: **How does God's vision compare with the way we usually attempt to do missionary work?**

Say: **In order to accomplish the worldwide task God has given to us, we need to be informed about our world issues that pose challenges to the spread of the Gospel. But how can we gather pertinent information in an efficient manner?** As a group, brainstorm specific ways to gather information about the world and what God is doing in it. List responses on the chalkboard. Encourage members to think beyond the suggestions in the text. For example,when someone mentions eating in an ethnic restaurant, make a list of such local eating places that members are familiar with. Or when missionary letters or reports are mentioned, have members name the missionaries your congregation supports, and tell what they know about them and their ministries.

Comment that there are many excellent publications available today to inform us about missionary activities in the world. Show and explain the resources you brought, then pass them around the group. Allow time for members to examine them; encourage everyone to note titles and publications they find especially interesting and tell them where such literature can be found. Take time to read excerpts from *Operation World*.

Say: **Another source of information is television. Let's take a few minutes to find out what is available this week, for example.** Encourage everyone who brought television guides for the week to share them with someone who did not. Instruct members to look through the listings and mark specials on other cultures and international events. The public television station probably will be the best source. If you are short of time, assign different days of the week to different people. After they report to the others on what they found, promote these programs.

Say: **News programs and daily newspapers are other good sources of information and issues.** Instruct those who brought the news sections of recent newspapers to share sections so everyone has one. Give the group a few minutes to skim through the articles. Then ask volunteers to identify local, national, or international events that impact God's program around the world and how these events affect missions.

Say: **In addition to news and culture information, we need to be aware of major issues that challenge the spread of worldwide Christianity.** Briefly review the mega-issues as outlined in chapter 4 of the text. Ask members for any additional suggestions.

Applying the Truth   *(5-8 minutes)*

Say: **The task of gathering information about the world, God's activities in it, and issues that confront us can be overwhelming. But the author of our text has suggested several practical steps to get started: Pray, start a file, read recent books, talk with cross-cultural friends, attend seminars, and pool information.** List each suggestion on the chalkboard as you name it, and elaborate as necessary.

Then have everyone choose one area of interest, such as a country, a people group, or an issue. Challenge members to begin information gathering this week by taking the first two or three steps on the chalkboard.

Close with prayer, asking God to make His vision for the world that of every member.

ASSIGNMENT

1. Ask members to prepare to share at the next session one piece of information they gathered about the world or missions during the week.
2. Instruct them to read chapter 5 of the text.

A LOOK AT WORLD-CLASS PRAYERS

TEXT, CHAPTER 5

Session Topic
God uses our prayers to accomplish His work around the world.

Session Goals
1. To describe a world-class prayer.
2. To discover the content of world-class prayers and find reasons for praying in this manner.
3. To pray for requests related to God's work in the world.

Materials Needed
√ Bible
√ *How to Be a World-Class Christian*
√ Sheets of poster board
√ Paper, pencils, pairs of scissors
√ Rulers, markers for small groups
√ Chalkboard and chalk

Special Preparation
1. As you prepare, read about prayer in *Daring to Draw Near* by John White and *The God Who Hears* by W. Bingham Hunter, both from InterVarsity Press. White's book studies prayers of the Bible, including those of Hannah and Paul which are included in this session. Hunter's book will help you wrestle with the question, "Why pray, since God is sovereign?"
2. As you prepare, think about this challenge:

   Prayer, missions, and evangelism are interrelated because prayer brings us face to face with God and His plans....

We must pray in order to face the unfinished task of world evangelism. We must pray if we desire to build a personal world vision. The need, the opportunity, and the Lord all drive us to our knees. And as we pray we will see the powerful ways in which God works, even ways that we do not know or understand.

Through our prayers, God allows us to be part of His changing the world (Paul Borthwick, *A Mind for Missions*, NavPress, 1987, p. 63).

3. Prior to the session, write on the chalkboard the list of names and references in *Discovering God's Principles*.

LESSON PLAN

Launching the Lesson   *(15–20 minutes)*

Say: **During the past few sessions, we've explored the meaning of the term *world-class* as it describes a Christian. Today we want to relate it to prayer. To get us thinking about world-class prayer, I'd like you to write print ads for it.**

Divide members into groups of five and appoint leaders. Give groups poster board, blank paper, markers, pencils, a scissors, and a ruler. Instruct them to make posters advertising world-class prayer. Tell them to think about what it would include and exclude. Encourage groups to get across the key ideas in world-class prayer. If you will not have enough time for this activity, discuss it as a group instead; or start the activity as members arrive.

Reassemble everyone and have the leader from each group show and read its ad. Say: **Let's see how our ads compare with some world-class prayers in the Bible.**

Discovering God's Principles   *(30–35 minutes)*

Divide the group into six study groups with leaders, and distribute paper and pencils. Give each group one of the following "pray-ers" and the related Scriptures, found on the board:

- *Moses* (Ex. 15:1-18)
- *Hannah* (1 Sam. 2:1-10)
- *Solomon* (1 Kings 8:22-34, 41-43, 56-61)
- *Nebuchadnezzar* (Dan. 4:28-37)
- *Jesus* (John 17:13-26)

■ *Paul* (Eph. 1:15-23; 3:14-21)

Instruct the groups to study their prayers, recording what they learn about God and His view of the world. Then have them think of specific ways to apply those truths to our prayers today.

When everyone is finished, reassemble and call for reports. Members may take notes as they hear reports from other groups. Ask:

■ *What elements do these biblical prayers have in common?*
■ *How do they compare with our prayers?*

Discuss: **One truth that stands out in these prayers is that God is sovereign; He is in control of the world. Since this is so, why should we bother to pray?** Let members wrestle with this question for a few minutes. Point out that God uses prayer to mold and change us, that prayer makes us partners with Him in His program throughout the world, and that prayer enables Christians to have victory in the spiritual warfare they are engaged in.

Wrap up by reading Borthwick's quote in *Special Preparation.*

Applying the Truth   *(10–15 minutes)*

Say: **Since God has allowed us to be partners with Him through prayer, let's use this privilege.** Ask members to relate prayer requests for countries and people groups that they have been gathering information about during the week, for missionaries that members know, for current events that impact the spread of the Gospel, and for personal needs in relation to this study. Include the country for the day in *Operation World* by summarizing some of the information about it and its needs. Ask a member to jot down the prayer requests and needs on the chalkboard so that none will be forgotten. Take time for conversational prayer for these requests, encouraging members to pray world-class prayers.

Urge them to keep praying world-class prayers all week.

ASSIGNMENT

---

1. Encourage members with copies of *Operation World* to use them daily during the coming week.
2. Have them consider obstacles they meet praying for others.
3. Instruct everyone to read chapter 5 of the text.

OUR PRAYERS CAN BE WORLD-CLASS

TEXT, CHAPTER 6

Session Topic

Through prayer we can help others who are serving God around the world.

Session Goals

1. To identify steps involved in learning new skills.
2. To explore reasons for praying for others worldwide and to list steps to getting started.
3. To set goals for increasing global praying.

Materials Needed

√ Bible
√ *How to Be a World-Class Christian*
√ Note cards, pencils
√ Missionary prayer letters and prayer cards
√ Bible references on slips of paper (see *Special Preparation #1*)
√ Chalkboard and chalk

Special Preparation

1. On separate slips of paper, write the following Scripture references: Ephesians 1:15-19a; 3:16-19; Philippians 1:9-11; Colossians 1:9-12; and Philemon 6. Repeat the sequence until you have slips enough for all members.
2. Ask your church secretary or missions committee chairman for copies of the latest letters from the missionaries the church supports. Make enough photocopies to give each member one. Also collect available prayer cards.

LESSON PLAN

Launching the Lesson   (5 minutes)

Have members think of new skills they have learned, such as playing the piano, playing tennis, or painting. Ask them to identify the steps involved in learning that skill. Then say: **Some of these same steps apply to becoming world-class "pray-ers," our topic for today.**

Discovering God's Principles   (25–30 minutes)

State that before you examine the steps involved, you will review the importance of praying for others. Ask: **Why is it important to pray for people who are involved in the task of world evangelization?** List responses on the chalkboard under the heading "WHY PRAY?" as members look up these verses:

- *Romans 15:30-32*. (So that those working in world evangelism will be freed from persecution that hinders the teaching of God's Word and be free to accomplish His will.)
- *2 Corinthians 1:8-11*. (So they will be delivered from trials beyond their ability to endure.)
- *Ephesians 6:18-20*. (So they will speak the Gospel boldly; that their ministry will be effective.)
- *Philippians 1:12-20*. (So those working in world evangelism will be delivered from physical imprisonment and so Christ will be exalted in their lives.)
- *Colossians 4:2-4*. (So God will open doors for the Gospel to be proclaimed and His workers will speak it clearly.)
- *2 Thessalonians 3:1*. (So God's word will spread rapidly and be honored by those who hear it.)

Ask: **Which of these reasons for praying for those in world evangelism surprised you? Why?**

Summarize: **We have a great privilege and responsibility to pray for others. But it is often difficult to pray consistently in the world-class manner we studied in the last session. What are some of the obstacles we face as we desire to pray for others worldwide?** List these on the chalkboard as members give them under the heading "OBSTACLES." Then ask members to suggest some practical ways of overcoming each obstacle. List these ways across from the corresponding obstacles and under the heading "RESPONSES."

Say: **The author of our text outlines 10 specific steps to starting to build our global prayer lives.** Review these with the group, asking for personal examples.

Applying the Truth   *(5–8 minutes)*

Read the last paragraph in chapter 6 of the text as a challenge to your members. Then ask: **What are *you* going to do to get the job done?** Distribute note cards and pencils. Instruct members to write one or two goals for their growth in global praying plus several steps to accomplish each goal. Have them put a check mark by the one they will work on this week.

Prayer Time   *(10–15 minutes)*

Say: **Let's begin our global praying with prayer for some of the missionaries our congregation supports.** Have members form pairs or triads. Give everyone a copy of a missionary prayer letter and/or prayer card plus a slip of paper with the reference of one of Paul's prayers. Ask everyone to read the letter and the biblical prayer. Members will then pray in pairs or triads those same prayers for their missionaries along with other requests noted in the letters.

ASSIGNMENT

1. Instruct members to put the prayer goals sheet in a place where they will see it often and follow through.
2. Encourage everyone to use Paul's prayers as patterns for praying for people involved in spreading the Gospel.
3. Instruct members to read chapter 7 of the text.

Planning Ahead

For session 9, you will invite one or two internationals to talk briefly about the problems they encountered when they came to this country. Begin now to locate someone. See *Special Preparation* in session 9 for details.

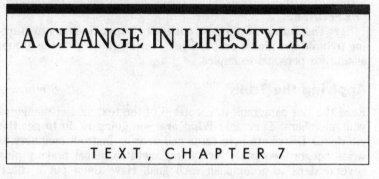

A CHANGE IN LIFESTYLE

T E X T ,   C H A P T E R   7

Session Topic
World-class Christians simplify their lifestyles.

Session Goals
1. To contrast our lifestyles with those of the rest of the world.
2. To discover biblical principles for our lifestyles and ways to simplify them.
3. To assess our lifestyles, covenanting with God to simplify.

Materials Needed
√ Bible
√ *How to Be a World-Class Christian*
√ Pictures, construction paper; slides or taped commercials
√ Equipment for a slide/video show (optional)
√ Recording of "Things" (Scott Wesley Brown, *To the Ends of the Earth,* Word); CD or tape player
√ Paper, pencils
√ Chalkboard and chalk

Special Preparation
1. Locate ads or pictures of people suffering in other lands (i.e., the homeless; the starving; sick children.) Also find ads that say, in essence, "You're worth it"; or "You've earned it." Find at least ten pictures in all. Mount them on construction paper, alternating suffering pictures with "you're-worth-it" pictures. If you have the time and equipment, take slides of such ads or videotape TV commercials. Show these with background music, such as "Dying People" (Harvest, *Holy Fire,* Benson).

2. Prior to the session, write on the chalkboard the principles and references found in *Discovering God's Principles*.
3. Spend time evaluating your lifestyle and the grip that things have on you. Write your Zaccheus covenant with God prior to the session (see *Applying the Truth*). If you feel. comfortable doing so, read it to the group as a sample.

LESSON PLAN

Launching the Lesson   (5–10 minutes)

Show the pictures or videotaped commercials. Ask for members' reactions to these very different lifestyles and attitudes. Say: **We're surrounded by messages which tell us to buy things we don't need and which perpetuate our materialism. In contrast, most of the world lives in abject poverty. J. Herbert Kane, in his book *Wanted: World Christians* (Baker Book House, 1986, pp. 188–89), explains the situation through this illustration:**

> If we could compress the total population of the world, which now [in 1986] stands at 4.8 billion persons, into a community of 1,000 persons living in a single town, the following picture of contrasts would emerge: 60 persons would represent the population of the United States; the remainder of the world would be represented by 940 persons. The 60 Americans would be receiving half the total income of the entire community; the other 940 persons would have to share the remaining half.
>
> The 60 Americans would have 15 times as many possessions per person as the others. . . .
>
> Most of the 940 non-Americans in the community would always be hungry, most of them poor, ignorant, illiterate, and sick. Half of them would be unable to read or write. Half of them would never have heard of Jesus Christ.

Continue: **In light of these inequities, let's explore what God says about a world-class lifestyle.**

Discovering God's Principles   (30–35 minutes)

Refer to the chalkboard and point out that the author of the text highlights stewardship, sacrifice, and solidarity as they relate to lifestyle. Distribute paper and pencils. Divide the members into three groups and assign each group one of the following principles and its references:

- *Stewardship* (Ps. 24:1; Matt. 6:19-21; Mark 4:18-19; 1 Tim. 6:17-20)
- *Sacrifice* (Luke 21:1-4; 2 Cor. 8:1-5)
- *Solidarity* (Deut. 15:7-8; Prov. 19:17; Isa. 58:6-10; Heb. 13:3)

Instruct members to use the passages and text to write, individually or with their neighbors, descriptions of a world-class lifestyle. Any who finish early may study another section.

When everyone is done, call for responses. Discuss: **Why is exercising these qualities vital in being world-class believers?**

Summarize by reading this quote from the text: **"The biblical bottom line: Jesus calls us to respond to what we know through simplifying our lifestyles."** Discuss: **What are some realistic steps we can take to simplify our lifestyles?** Supplement members' answers with suggestions from the text, if necessary.

Applying the Truth   *(10–20 minutes)*

If you have time, play a recording of the song "Things," asking members to reflect on their own lifestyles as they listen.

Say: **To be world-class Christians, we must evaluate the possessions we own or want, then deliberately choose not to accumulate more.** Read the second-to-last paragraph of chapter 7, beginning with "We can choose. . . . " Ask: **Are you willing to take the challenge?** Have some silent prayer time as members talk to God about changes in their lifestyles He wants them to make.

Distribute sheets of paper and tell members to title them "Covenant." Tell them to review the Zaccheus Covenant (chapter 7 of the text, under the heading "Principle: Chosen Hardship), then to spend the rest of the session time writing their own covenants with God.

ASSIGNMENT

1. Urge members to review their covenants throughout the week and determine to follow through on their commitments.
2. Ask members to review the amount of their fiscal giving in light of their incomes and the recipients of the giving.
3. Have everyone read chapter 8 of the text.

MONEY: AT THE HEART OF THE MATTER

TEXT, CHAPTER 8

Session Topic
World-class Christians give generously and responsibly.

Session Goals
1. To illustrate common attitudes toward giving.
2. To examine biblical attitudes and characteristics of giving.
3. To evaluate our own attitudes and habits in giving with the goal of aligning them with biblical teaching.

Materials Needed
√ Bible
√ *How to Be a World-Class Christian*
√ Copies of Response Sheet 4, pencils
√ Poster board, marker, paper
√ Topical concordance and/or chain reference Bible
√ Chalkboard and chalk

Special Preparation
1. Using a topical concordance and/or chain reference Bible, do a study in both testaments on giving. Find out what the rest of Scripture adds to Paul's instructions to the Corinthians. Ask yourself what changes you need to make in your own attitudes toward giving and in your actions of giving before you try to teach these principles to your group.
2. Using a marker, print out the verse 1 Chronicles 29:14 in large letters on a sheet of poster board.

LESSON PLAN

Launching the Lesson   *(15–20 minutes)*

Divide members into three groups and appoint leaders. Instruct each group to plan and present a two- or three-minute dialogue that depicts typical attitudes toward giving that believers have. Dialogues may have dramatic or creative presentations if the group so chooses. Give each group paper and pencils for notes.

After about 8–10 minutes, reassemble and have each group present its dialogue. Then say: **Giving tends to be a volatile subject for believers, as illustrated by the attitudes we've just observed. Today we want to focus on making God's attitude toward giving our own as we grow as world-class Christians.**

Discovering God's Principles   *(25–35 minutes)*

Share the following with the group: **Second Corinthians 8–9 contains an extensive discussion on giving. But before studying this passage, we should be aware of certain background information. Paul was in the process of raising money in Gentile churches to help Jewish believers in Jerusalem who were poverty-stricken. He began the collection referred to in 2 Corinthians a year earlier; in fact, he first mentioned it in 1 Corinthians 16. But due to internal problems, the Corinthians had not followed through. So then he urged them to complete their collection so it could be delivered to those who needed the money. Note that this was a cross-cultural giving situation.**

Say: **Now let's look at 2 Corinthians 8–9 to see what Paul taught about world-class giving.** Have members work in the same three groups as before. Distribute pencils and copies of Response Sheet 4 and assign each group one section of the passage. Instruct groups to complete their parts of the Bible study chart. State that the group taking 2 Corinthians 9:6-15 will note the results of both the right and wrong attitudes/actions. Mention that not all topics will apply to each passage.

While the groups are working, draw the same chart on the chalkboard, leaving enough space to record answers. When the groups are finished, reassemble and call for reports. Fill in the chalkboard chart, encouraging members to complete their response sheets. Use the following information as needed:

1 Corinthians 16:1-2; 2 Corinthians 8:1-6

Right attitudes/actions: Joyful, generous giving—in proportion to income, as much as one is able—even more; sacrificial giving; giving oneself to the Lord first; giving regarded as a privilege. Regularly setting something aside; taking personal responsibility.

Motives: Service to others.

2 Corinthians 8:7-15

Right attitudes/actions: Willingness; giving according to what one has—not according to what one does not have.

Motives: Love; Christ's sacrifice for us; equality.

Results: Gift is acceptable to God; equality among believers (meets their needs).

2 Corinthians 9:6-15

Wrong attitudes/actions: Sparing and reluctant giving, as if under compulsion.

Results: Few returns.

Right attitudes/actions: Generous and cheerful giving; personal responsibility.

Motives: Obedience to God.

Results: Generous returns; pleasing God, knowing His grace; the giver will have what he needs, plus increased means to give and greater righteousness; thanksgiving in others; the meeting of others' needs; praise to God.

Lead a discussion by asking:

■ *What is the relationship between what God has done for us and our giving to spread the Gospel around the world?*

■ *How does generosity affect our own attitudes? Our perspective? Our worship? The world?*

Display your poster of 1 Chronicles 29:14 and read this verse as a group. Ask: **How should this verse transform our giving?**

Applying the Truth   *(8–10 minutes)*

Ask members to reflect on their own giving habits and attitudes in light of what Paul taught the Corinthian believers. Ask:

■ *How do your attitudes compare with the ones God says we should have as we give?*

■ *Are you giving regularly? Generously in proportion to your income?*

■ *What changes do you need to make in your giving in order to grow as a world-class Christian?*

Have members record any changes God is prompting them to make on the back of their response sheets along with specific steps toward achieving those changes that they can take this week.

Allow a few minutes of silent prayer as members talk to God about their giving attitudes and habits; then close the session.

ASSIGNMENT

1. Encourage members to begin working on one or two steps toward the change(s) they listed in *Applying the Truth*.
2. Have members take note during the week of the numbers and nationalities of internationals whom they contact at work or see in stores or around their neighborhoods.
3. Tell members to read chapter 9 of the text.

REACHING THE WORLD THAT HAS COME TO US

TEXT, CHAPTER 9

Session Topic

World-class Christian involvement starts by reaching out to the world God has brought to us.

Session Goals

1. To become aware of the problems internationals face in our country.
2. To explore why we should minister to internationals.
3. To identify ways of ministering to internationals and pray about our involvement with them.

Materials Needed

√ Bible
√ *How to Be a World-Class Christian*
√ Taped interviews, tape player (optional)
√ Poster board, rulers, a good supply of colored markers
√ Tables
√ Paper, pencils, pairs of scissors, glue
√ Chalkboard and chalk

Special Preparation

1. Invite one or two internationals to speak to your group for five minutes each about the problems they faced when they came to your country. If you do not have anyone in your church, call some neighboring congregations, local hospitals, or large companies in your area. Try to find people from different countries who immigrated for a variety of reasons if you have time for more than one person to speak. If it is impossible to schedule

someone to come to the session, arrange to tape-record comments ahead of time. Plan to give any guest who is not from your church a small honorarium for his or her time. If you cannot find anyone with whom to talk, look for magazine articles or books that relate personal testimonies and read excerpts to the group.

2. Explore the possibilities for ministry with internationals in your community so you can make concrete suggestions to group members who are interested. Talk with your pastor, local colleges, and social services agencies.

3. Before the session starts, write these references on the chalkboard: Exodus 22:21; Leviticus 19:33-34; Deuteronomy 10:17-19; 16:10-14; Psalm 96; and Hebrews 13:1-2.

4. Set up tables where members can work on their recruitment posters (see *Discovering God's Principles*). For each table, supply a sheet of poster board, paper, pencils, scissors, glue, colored markers, and a ruler.

LESSON PLAN

Launching the Lesson   (15–20 minutes)

Introduce your international guests and ask them to tell briefly about their adjustments, problems, and fears when they came to your country. Allow a few minutes for members to ask questions. Or, if you tape-recorded interviews beforehand, play the tape.

Do not be upset if your guests speak longer than you asked them to. The point is that they are your guests and you want them to feel welcome. Since this session deals with ministry to internationals among us, this is the very place to minister to them. Thank them for their time and for sharing from their personal histories. Consider ways to keep in contact with your guests so that they do not feel "dropped" once their sharing time is over.

Say: **It isn't easy for internationals to come to live in this country; but because of these very problems, we have ready opportunities of cross-cultural ministry without leaving our homes. Today we want to focus on why we should get involved with internationals and how we can effectively minister to them.**

Discovering God's Principles   *(30–40 minutes)*

Tell the members they will explore what God's Word says about ministering to strangers among them. Divide members into groups of four or five, appoint leaders, and have them be seated at the tables. Assign the passages you wrote on the board as evenly as possible among the groups. They should read the verses and locate the actions and considerations that should be shown to aliens plus the attitudes that are prescribed. After groups have finished working, call for reports.

Next, instruct each group to make a recruitment poster for ministering to internationals living in your country. In addition to communicating the truths found in the passages they just studied, the groups should also include contemporary examples.

When groups have finished working, reassemble everyone. Have the leader from each group show and read its poster. (After the session, display the posters in the church building or meeting place where the rest of your congregation can read them.)

Say: **Ministering to strangers among us is a significant way to reach the world without ever leaving home. But it is not always easy, as Scripture attests. Let's look at a familiar passage that illustrates this fact, Luke 10:25-37.** Have members turn to this section and read it individually. Ask: **What are some of the costs of helping our international neighbors?** (Possible rejection [Samaritans were despised by the Jewish people]; time, material goods, money, ourselves.) **So why should we help even though it's costly?** (Because God told us to love our neighbors — including internationals.)

Also refer members to the story of Philip and the Ethiopian eunuch (Acts 8:26-40). After they read the passage, ask: **What resulted from the faithfulness of Philip to witness to this international?** (Rejoicing, the Ethiopian returned to his own land as a believer, perhaps to become a witness himself.)

If you have time, ask any members who have been involved with internationals to share their experiences — both rewards and frustrations.

Applying the Truth   *(10 minutes)*

Brainstorm this question: **What are some specific ways we can reach out to internationals in our area?** List responses on the board. Encourage members to focus on what is practical and possible where you live, not just to reiterate what the text says.

Say: **There are lots of opportunities to be missionaries right here — if we are willing to follow through on these suggestions. The first step is to pray, asking God what He wants us to do as individuals and as a group.** Spend some time in prayer doing just that. If the prayertime reveals a common interest or burden among some, encourage those members to talk during the week to plan for action.

ASSIGNMENT

1. Ask members to pray daily about their part in reaching internationals.
2. In preparation for the next session, ask members to think about risks they have taken recently and what the results were.
3. Tell members to reflect on how God has changed their perspectives about Christian living as they have sought to grow as world-class believers.
4. Instruct everyone to read chapter 10 of the text.

GOING GLOBAL

TEXT, CHAPTER 10

Session Topic
Experiences in other cultures introduce us to risks and deepen our growth as world-class Christians.

Session Goals
1. To tell about risks you have taken.
2. To examine one of Paul's cross-cultural risks and identify ones you can take to grow as world-class believers.
3. To set a high-risk goal and identify steps to reach it.

Materials Needed
√ Bible
√ *How to Be a World-Class Christian*
√ A two-foot length of aluminum foil for each member
√ Risk Plan sheets from Visual Sketch 1, pencils
√ Chalkboard and chalk

Special Preparation
1. Note Paul's risks in Acts 13–28 and 2 Corinthians 11:16-33.
2. Copy Visual Sketch 1 on a blank sheet of typing paper and make enough copies for your group.

LESSON PLAN

Building the Body
(5–10 minutes)

Ask members how God has changed their perspectives about the Christian life as they've grown as world-class believers.

Launching the Lesson (10–15 minutes)

Hand out two-foot pieces of aluminum foil to the group. Instruct members to tear out or sculpt an object that illustrates some kind of risk they have taken (for example, sharing their faith with a neighbor, riding a roller coaster, getting a new haircut, skydiving).

After five minutes, everyone will show and briefly explain his or her sculpture, you included. If your group is larger, divide it into two groups so that everyone will have a chance to share.

Say: **Taking risks is a part of living. Some risks may be small, like _____ (refer to a member's sculpture); others are quite daring, like _____ (again refer to a specific sculpture). Experiencing other cultures as world-class Christians involves risks too, as we shall discover in this session.**

Discovering God's Principles (20–25 minutes)

Tell the group: **One of the greatest cross-cultural risk-takers was the Apostle Paul. We've already examined some of his experiences. Let's look at another.** Have members turn to Acts 17:13-34, and ask one or two volunteers to read this passage aloud.

State that Paul had not gone to Athens specifically to minister; rather, it was a stopover point. Ask:

■ *But how did Paul feel regarding the city? Why?* (He was distressed because there were so many idols, indicating that the people did not know the true God.)

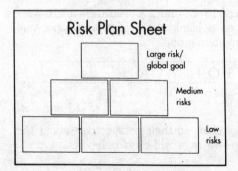

Risk Plan Sheet

Large risk/global goal

Medium risks

Low risks

Visual Sketch 1
A specific plan for growth will help members work up to high risk, global involvement.

■ *How does his reaction compare to ours when we visit a new city?* (While we are usually interested in sightseeing, he was primarily interested in the spiritual condition of the people. He did, however, look around the city to find out what he could about the people, as we read in verse 23.)

■ *What did Paul do as a result of seeing their idols?* (He talked to people about the Lord both in the synagogue and the marketplace.)

■ *How did he relate his message to his audience?* (He explained that the unknown God they already worshiped is the God of creation who calls men to repentance. He also knew enough about Greek culture to incorporate a line from one of their poets into his message.)

■ *What happened as a result of Paul's witnessing to various groups in the city?* (Some wanted to hear more, some sneered, and some believed.)

■ *What kinds of risks did Paul take in Athens?* (Having the Jews stir up the people against him and threaten his life; being ignored or run out of town.)

■ *Why did Paul take these risks?* (His commitment to being a world-class believer was greater than his concern for his personal happiness and welfare.)

Say: **Yes, it is risky to reach out to other cultures. But God doesn't usually ask us to start with the high risks Paul experienced as a missionary. We can start going global on a smaller scale and work up to higher risks.** Label three columns on the chalkboard LOW RISKS, MEDIUM RISKS, HIGH RISKS. Ask members to identify specific examples of each degree of risk that are appropriate and possible for them to take. (For example, low risk—reading about other cultures; medium risk—befriending someone from another culture; high risk—inviting that friend to church with you.) List responses on the board.

Discuss: **What are some of the results we can expect from taking any of these risks?** Ask for testimonies from individuals who have done so. Also review what the text presents.

Applying the Truth   *(10 minutes)*

Challenge members by reading the last paragraph of chapter 10 of the text. Then say: **But taking risks is not automatic, nor does it come naturally. We need to plan for growth in this area.** Distribute pencils and copies of the Risk Plan sheets that you made from

Visual Sketch 1. Instruct members to think and pray about a long-range, global goal (such as a summer/short term missions project; teaching English as a second language; inviting an international with a housing need to live in your home) and write it in the last column. Then have them break the goal down into steps that start with low risks and progress toward that high-risk goal. If people are not ready to set high-risk goals now, have them take the sheet home and continue to pray until God gives them a high-risk goal with global implications.

Close with prayer.

ASSIGNMENT

1. Encourage members to begin meeting one of their low-risk goals this week.
2. Have members read chapter 11 of the text.

NEARSIGHTEDNESS

TEXT, CHAPTER 11

Session Topic

A commitment to world-class outreach begins by paying attention to the needs around us.

Session Goals

1. To evaluate our commitment to local outreach.
2. To identify the biblical pattern for outreach, and ways we can follow it.
3. To select one way to be a local witness.

Materials Needed

✓ Bible
✓ *How to Be a World-Class Christian*
✓ Copies of Response Sheet 5, pencils
✓ Large map of Bible lands; books on evangelism
✓ Recording of "People Need the Lord" sung by Steve Green (*Steve Green*, Sparrow); CD or tape player (optional)
✓ Poster board or newsprint, markers
✓ Chalkboard and chalk

Special Preparation

1. On a Bible atlas, learn to locate the places named in the Acts study in *Discovering God's Principles*.
2. Gather books on evangelism from your church library and/or your pastor. Choose from titles in chapter 11 of the text plus: *How to Give Away Your Faith* by Paul Little (InterVarsity Press); *Say It With Love* by Howard G. Hendricks (Victor); *The Non-Confronter's Guide to Leading a Person to Christ* by Walter

S. Bleeker (Here's Life); *Evangelism: A Biblical Approach* by G. Michael Cocoris (Moody Press); *Your Home — A Lighthouse* by Bob and Betty Jacks with Ron Wormser, Sr., (NavPress).

LESSON PLAN

Building the Body   *(5–10 minutes)*

Going around the group, have each member say briefly who told him or her about salvation in Jesus Christ and that person's relationship to the member (i.e., friend, relative, pastor, stranger). When everyone has participated, including yourself, note the percentage who became believers because of people who lived close to them.

Launching the Lesson   *(10 minutes)*

Distribute pencils and copies of Response Sheet 5. Instruct members to evaluate their spiritual nearsightedness by answering the statements honestly; no one else will see their answers.

When members are done, ask them for their reactions to the statements and to their scores. Then say: **Doing this exercise may sting us some, especially since we've been trying to develop a greater interest and involvement in the world. But sometimes we focus so much on the whole world that we ignore or forget the needs all around us. Today we want to focus our vision closer to home.**

Discovering God's Principles   *(25–30 minutes)*

State that the group will review how the early church followed the principle of ministering to those in its immediate vicinity. Have members turn to Acts 1:6-8, and ask a volunteer to read these verses aloud. Ask: **What geographical strategy of evangelism did Jesus outline to His disciples?** (First, they should go to Jerusalem, the city in which they lived; then to Judea and Samaria, the disciples' own country; then to the ends of the earth, the rest of the world.) As responses are given, draw on the chalkboard three concentric circles, labeling the inner circle *city*, the middle circle *country*, and the outer circle *world*. Also draw an arrow from the center outward.

Say: **Let's see how the disciples carried out Jesus' command.** Display the map of Bible lands where all can see it. As members

read aloud the following verses from Acts, point out on the map
the locations they mention.

- *1:12* (Jerusalem)
- *2:5* (Jerusalem)
- *3:1* (Jerusalem, site of the temple)
- *4:1* (Jerusalem)
- *5:12* (Jerusalem — Solomon's colonnade was a section in the
  outer court of the temple.)
- *8:1* (Judea and Samaria)
- *8:5* (Samaria)
- *8:26* (Toward Gaza on the coast of Judea)
- *8:40* (Azotus in Judea to Caèsarea in Samaria)
- *9:32* (Around the country)
- *10:1* (Caesarea in Samaria)
- *11:19* (Phoenicia, Cyprus, and Antioch, outside Judea and
  Samaria)

Point out that the rest of the Book of Acts is the story of evangelism outside Israel.

Say: **We Christians often have an inverted vision of where
and how Christ wants us to minister. Why is it easier for us to
be more concerned about the rest of the world than the area
where we live?** (Many have a mental image of missions which
includes only cultures and lands far away. Some believers are
attracted to the "glamour" of overseas missions, but not by the
prospect of serving in their neighborhoods.)

Say: **At other times we don't witness to those around us because we don't know what to say or are afraid of what their
reactions might be. But Jesus promised us the power to be His
witnesses, beginning at home. And there are plenty of resources available to help us in this task.** Show and briefly review
the books on evangelism you gathered. Pass them around, encouraging everyone to borrow or buy at least one and read it.

Discuss: **Why is it important for world-class Christians to be
committed to serving in their local congregations before moving
out into the rest of the world?** Add any reasons from the text that
are omitted. When someone mentions the fact that it is a training
ground for global service, ask members to name specific ministries
in your church that can prepare them for worldwide service, and
tell how the ministries can do so.

Ask: **How does local church involvement add credibility to a
person's desire to serve God in another location?** (A person who

is willing to serve in the ordinary, day-to-day surroundings of the local church shows that ministering is more important to him or her than where it is done.)

Say: **As much as we need to be witnesses where we are, there is a real danger in being so nearsighted that we lose our vision for the rest of the world. How can we keep ourselves and our church from turning inward?** Push members to be specific and practical.

Applying the Truth   (5 minutes)

Say: **There is an old saying that is very appropriate for today's topic: Bloom where you are planted. God wants us to be witnesses where He has planted us now, as well as to develop a burden for the whole world. How well are you blooming here in _____ (name your city)? In what ways do you need to enlarge your vision for your "Jerusalem?"** Have members look at their response sheets again. Instruct them to place a star in front of one "no" statement to work on this week.

Optional: If you have time, play the song "People Need the Lord" as a challenge to tell the people we meet about salvation through Jesus Christ.

Prayer Time   (5 minutes)

Have members pair up, share their goals for the week, and pray for each other.

ASSIGNMENT

1. Encourage members to write their prayer partners' goals on the back of the response sheet and pray daily for them during the week.
2. Ask members to think about this question: If you could personally ask God three questions, what would they be?
3. Have members read chapter 12 of the text.

GOD CALLS WORLDWIDE

TEXT, CHAPTER 12

Session Topic
God may call some of us to global ministry.

Session Goals
1. To make members aware of the level of their own concern for knowing God's will.
2. To discover how God calls people to global ministry.
3. To select one way to move towards global ministry now.

Materials Needed
√ Bible
√ *How to Be a World-Class Christian*
√ Note cards, pencils; poster board, markers
√ Recording of one of these songs: "Lord of the Harvest" (Imperials, *Stand by the Power,* Day Spring); "If We Don't Believe (Send Us to the World)" (Harvest, *Send Us to the World,* Milk & Honey); "Go" (Harvest, *Holy Fire,* Benson); "Send Me" (Twila Paris, *Same Girl,* Star Song); "Please Don't Send Me to Africa" (Scott Wesley Brown, *To the Ends of the Earth,* Word); CD or tape player
√ Chalkboard and chalk

Special Preparation
1. Scan *Decision Making and the Will of God* by Garry Friesen with J. Robin Maxson (Multnomah).
2. Talk with the chairperson of your missions committee and/or your pastor to learn what kinds of ministries your missionaries perform. Also check missions periodicals for more ideas.

3. Reproduce Visual Sketch 2 using poster board and markers.

LESSON PLAN

Launching the Lesson   *(8–10 minutes)*

Distribute note cards and pencils. Say: **If you could personally ask God three questions, what would they be?** Have members write down their questions without signing the cards. Collect the cards, shuffle them, and read the questions. Remark on the frequency (or lack) of questions related to knowing God's will. Then say: **Knowing God's will is one of the greatest concerns for believers in fellowship with Him. As we conclude these studies in becoming world-class Christians, we ought to be asking ourselves, "What is God's will for us? Is He calling us into another culture?" Today we want to consider this topic.**

Discovering God's Principles   *(20–25 minutes)*

Say to the group: **We can learn much about God's call to worldwide missionary service from Acts 13 where He called Barnabas and Saul, later known as Paul. Let's turn to this passage.** Have a volunteer read verses 1-5 aloud. Ask:

- *Who called Barnabas and Saul?* (The Holy Spirit)
- *Why did He choose these two men?* (They were already serving the Lord in a local congregation and had good reputations for being fruitful disciplers, evangelizers, and teachers, as we read in Acts 9:26-29; 11:25-26. They were devoted to the Lord, as evidenced by the fact that they were worshiping God and fasting.)

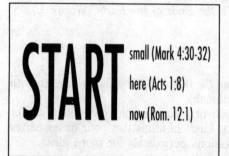

START small (Mark 4:30-32) here (Acts 1:8) now (Rom. 12:1)

Visual Sketch 2
Following these three steps will help us discern God's call to global ministry.

- *To whom did God make the missionary call known?* (The church leaders, who would have recognized the men's spiritual depth and abilities.)
- *How did the local church confirm God's call to Barnabas and Saul?* (The prophets and teachers of the church fasted and prayed, then laid their hands on Barnabas and Saul and sent them out.)
- *How did Barnabas and Saul respond?* (They left relatively quickly, obeying God's call.)
- *What did you learn about a missionary call from this passage?*
- *How does this pattern of calling for global ministry compare to what usually takes place today?*
- *Why do we tend to wait for individuals to announce their calls to missionary service rather than seeking God's leading for one another as a local body?*

Point out that this passage does not outline all the factors involved in determining God's call. Ask members to name some other contributing factors. Review the information in the text, asking for illustrations from members' own experiences.

Be sure to point out that knowing what opportunities are available and determining how our skills and education can be used in another part of the world also enter into determining our call to missions. In order to help members realize how God can use them, you may want to give a brief overview of the types of ministries the missionaries supported by your church perform.

Applying the Truth   *(20–25 minutes)*

Say: **The needs around the world are great. Matthew 9:37-38 is still true today.** Ask a volunteer to read these verses aloud.

Say: **If God is calling some of us, there are three practical ways we can find out.** Display the poster of Visual Sketch 2. One at a time, review each step by having someone read the Scripture verse, then asking the group for specific examples. Focus on what is applicable to your location and members' situations. Record suggestions on the chalkboard.

Have members prayerfully listen to a recording of one of the songs listed in *Materials Needed*.

Challenge members to start small, start here, and start now as they pray about God's will in worldwide ministry. Distribute note cards. Tell members to choose one way they will start here and now, and to write it down as a reminder.

Close with sentence prayers from the group.

ASSIGNMENT

1. Urge members to read their decision cards often during the week as a reminder to follow through.
2. Ask members to prepare to share the most important thing God taught them through this study and how He used the weekly assignments to help them change and grow.
3. Instruct members to read chapter 13 and review the rest of the text for the final session.

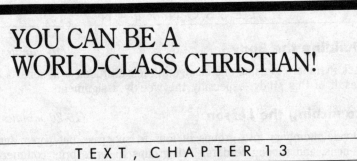

YOU CAN BE A
WORLD-CLASS CHRISTIAN!

TEXT, CHAPTER 13

Session Topic
Developing a growth plan helps us expand our worldwide vision.

Session Goals
1. To illustrate insights about world-class Christians.
2. To identify truths learned through this study and to make a poster to encourage continued growth.
3. To evaluate our growth as world-class believers and set goals for deepening our vision during the coming year.

Materials Needed
√ Bible
√ *How to Be a World-Class Christian*
√ Paper, pencils, markers for the group
√ Copies of Response Sheet 6
√ World-class Christian definition poster from session 2

Special Preparation
Reflect on how leading these studies has changed your life.

■ *What truths were especially helpful/challenging to you?*
■ *How have your attitudes changed toward world missions?*
■ *In what areas do you need to grow the most in order to deepen your world-class vision?*

LESSON PLAN

Building the Body
(10 minutes)

Ask members to name one change in their attitudes or actions as a result of this study, especially the weekly assignments.

Launching the Lesson
(15–20 minutes)

Divide members into groups of four to six, pass out paper and pencils, and appoint leaders. Tell groups to write brief commercials which advertise world-class Christians. Urge them to focus on descriptions, costs, and benefits. After 10–12 minutes, reassemble and have each small group present its commercial. Afterward, commend the groups for their creativity.

Discovering God's Principles
(15 minutes)

Ask members to identify the most important truth God taught them through this study. Be sure you participate too.

Say: **God has taught us a lot through this study. In order to encourage us to keep growing in this area, we're going to make individual posters.** Give each member a sheet of paper and a marker. Instruct everyone to create a poster that will encourage world-class growth. Emphasize that the members' posters should be meaningful and challenging to them. Suggest using one of the quotes that introduce the chapters of the text or a quote from the text itself. When all members have finished, let them read their posters to the group.

Applying the Truth
(15–20 minutes)

Say: **To keep our vision going and growing, we need to set goals to motivate and spur us toward becoming world-class Christians.** Display the definition poster. Distribute copies of Response Sheet 6 and instruct members to make growth goals for themselves for the next year. Have them use the text for suggestions in each area listed and record what they plan to do.

Close with a few minutes of conversational prayer, thanking God for specific insights and growth as a result of this study and asking for His help to continue to expand everyone's world-class visions. Ask one person to begin and another to close.

Response Sheet 1 Use with session 1 of *How to Be a WorldClass Christian.* © 1991 by SP Publications, Inc. Permission granted to purchaser to reproduce this Response Sheet for class purposes only.

PAUL: HAVE TRUTH, WILL TRAVEL

• •

How did Paul minister to the Thessalonians?

What were his attitudes toward them?

What were the results of his ministry with them?

What benefits did Paul personally experience as a result of being a world-class Christian?

WORLD-CLASS CHRISTIAN

"One whose lifestyle and Christian obedience is compatible, credible, and cooperative with what God is doing and wants to do in our world." (Borthwick)

How did he demonstrate that he was a world-class believer?

What obstacles did he have to overcome? How did he do so?

What were the results of his ministry?

Jesus
Matthew 11:1-6;
Mark 2:13-17;
Luke 7:36-50;
Acts 10:38

Ananias and
Barnabas
Acts 9:1-31

Peter
Acts 10:1-48

A LIVING OBITUARY

What would you, as a world-class Christian, want your obituary to say?

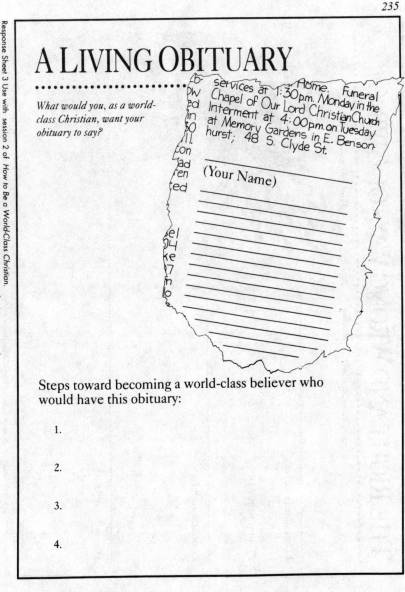

services at 1:30pm. Monday in the
Chapel of Our Lord ChristianChurch
Interment at 4:00pm. on Tuesday
at Memory Gardens in E. Benson-
hurst; 48 S. Clyde St.

(Your Name)

Steps toward becoming a world-class believer who would have this obituary:

1.

2.

3.

4.

THE RIGHT AND WRONG WAYS OF GIVING

Right Attitudes/Actions	Motives	Results	Wrong Attitudes/Actions	Results

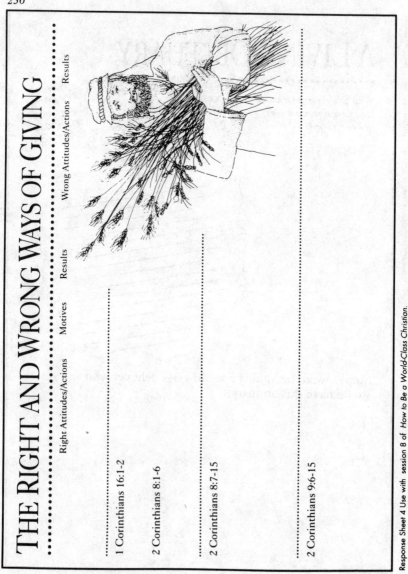

1 Corinthians 16:1-2

2 Corinthians 8:1-6

2 Corinthians 8:7-15

2 Corinthians 9:6-15

NEARSIGHTEDNESS TEST

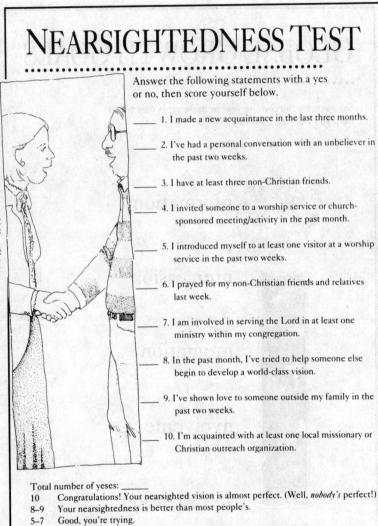

Answer the following statements with a yes or no, then score yourself below.

_____ 1. I made a new acquaintance in the last three months.

_____ 2. I've had a personal conversation with an unbeliever in the past two weeks.

_____ 3. I have at least three non-Christian friends.

_____ 4. I invited someone to a worship service or church-sponsored meeting/activity in the past month.

_____ 5. I introduced myself to at least one visitor at a worship service in the past two weeks.

_____ 6. I prayed for my non-Christian friends and relatives last week.

_____ 7. I am involved in serving the Lord in at least one ministry within my congregation.

_____ 8. In the past month, I've tried to help someone else begin to develop a world-class vision.

_____ 9. I've shown love to someone outside my family in the past two weeks.

_____ 10. I'm acquainted with at least one local missionary or Christian outreach organization.

Total number of yeses: _____

10   Congratulations! Your nearsighted vision is almost perfect. (Well, *nobody's* perfect!)

8–9   Your nearsightedness is better than most people's.

5–7   Good, you're trying.

2–4   You need to take a closer look at the people and needs around you.

0–1   Are you blind?

GLOBAL GROWTH GOALS

∙∙∙∙∙∙∙∙∙∙∙∙∙∙∙∙∙∙∙∙∙∙∙∙∙∙∙∙∙∙∙

Set goals for the coming year in these areas which will
help you become a world-class Christian.

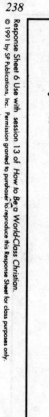

nformation

ntercession

ntegration

nvolvement

nvestigation

YOUR PART IN WORLD MISSIONS

You may be asking where you, as a Christian, fit into God's plan for the salvation of the world. Here are a few ways you can be involved now!

YOU CAN PRAY - Get informed about God's world. Ask for information about missionaries in areas of particular interest to you. Stand before God on behalf of your brothers and sisters on the mission field. Pray for more missionaries to be called and sent to reach the lost for Christ. Don't be surprised if God uses you to answer your own prayers.

YOU CAN GIVE - God has given you the priviledge of being responsible for a portion of His money. Decide how much you can keep for yourself, then use the rest to further God's kingdom. One way is to support foreign mission work.

YOU CAN SEND - Look around in your church or community. Seek out another who senses a call to missions, then spur that person on and encourage them to further seek God's direction for their life.

Adopt a missionary. Give him moral support. Encourage him through letters or tapes; let him know that you believe in him and in the work God has called him to. Maybe you are in the position to offer him a place to stay or a car to use while he's on home assignment.

YOU CAN GO - The great commission is a call to you too! You can see the need. Why delay?

MISSION AGENCIES AND THEIR ADDRESSES

African Inland Mission International in 23 countries
  USA PO Box 178, Pearl River, NY 10965
  800-254-0010
  e-mail: aim_info@aimint.org
  www.aim-us.org

Child Evangelism Fellowship in 60 countries
  USA PO Box 348, Warrenton, MO 63383
  800-300-4033
  e-mail: overseas@cefinc.org
  www.cefinc.org

Arab World Ministries in 24 countries
  USA PO Box 96, Upper Darby, PA 19082
  800-447-3566
  e-mail: awmusa@awm.org
  www.awm.com

Frontiers in 39 countries
  USA PO Box 31177, Mesa, AZ 85275-1177
  800-462-8436
  e-mail: info-us@frontiers.org
  www.frontiers.org

Greater Europe Mission in 21 countries
  USA 18950 Base Camp Rd, Monument, Co, 80132-8009
  800-436-4488
  e-mail: info@gemission.com
  www.gemission.org

Operation Mobilization in 80+ countries
  USA PO Box 444, Tyrone, GA 30290-0444
  770-631-0432
  e-mail: info@usa.om.org
  www.usa.om.org

Overseas Missionary Fellowship (OMF) in 21+ countries
        USA 10 W Dry Creek Circle, Littleton, CO 80120-4413
        800-993-2751
        e-mail: omfus@omf.org
        www.omf.org

SEND International in 12 countries
        USA PO Box 513, Farmington, MI 48332
        800-736-3808
        e-mail: sendus@send.org
        www.send.org

SIM International in 40 countires
        USA PO Box 7900, Charlotte, NC 28241-7900
        704-588-4300
        e-mail: info@sim.org
        www.sim.org

WEC International in 51 countries
        USA PO Box 1707, 709 Pennsylvania Ave.
                Fort Washington, PA   19034-8707
        888-646-6202
        e-mail: info@wec-usa.org
        www.wec-usa.org

Youth With A Mission (YWAM) in 106 Countries
        USA 7085 Battlecreek Rd SE, Salem, OR 97301
        503-364-3837
        e-mail: ywamnao@compuserve.com
        www.ywam.org

Other titles available from Gabriel Publishing...

Gabriel
Publishing

Contact us for details on any of these books -
PO Box 1047, Waynesboro, GA 30830
Tel: (706) 554-1594   Fax: (706) 554-7444
Toll-Free: 1-8MORE-BOOKS
e-mail: gabriel@omlit.om.org

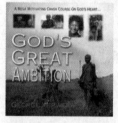

God's Great Ambition
Dan & Dave Davidson & George Verwer
ISBN: 1-884543-69-3

This unique collection of quotes and Scriptures has been designed to motivate thousands of people into action in world missions. George Verwer and the Davidsons are well-known for their ministries of mission mobilization as speakers and writers. Prepare to be blasted out of your comfort zone by this spiritual dynamite!

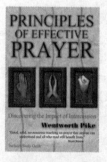

Principles of Effective Prayer
Wentworth Pike
ISBN: 1-884543-65-0

What is prayer? Why pray? Created as a devotional study for individuals or a textbook for groups, *Principles of Effective Prayer* answers these questions and many others. Developed as a class taught at Prairie Bible Institute (Canada), this book will lead you into a life and ministry of effective, God-glorifying prayer!

The Cross and The Crescent
Understanding the Muslim Heart and Mind
Phil Parshall
ISBN: 1-884543-68-5

Living as a missionary among Muslims, Phil Parshall understands the Muslim heart and mind. In this very personal book, he looks at what Muslims believe and how their beliefs affect - and don't affect - their behavior. He compares and contrasts Muslim and Christian views on the nature of God, sacred Scriptures, worship, sin and holiness, Jesus and Muhammed, human suffering, and the afterlife.

101 Ways to Change Your World
Geoff Tunnicliffe
ISBN: 1-884543-49-9

Geoff Tunnicliffe has compiled an invaluable collection of ways to change the world in his newly revised *101 Ways to Change Your World*. In addition to 101 practical ways to put faith into action, Tunnicliffe has also included statistics and resources for individuals desiring to make a difference in God's World.

Street Boy
Fletch Brown
ISBN: 1-884543-64-2

Jaime Jorka, a street boy in the Philippines, lays a challenge before the missionary whose wallet he has stolen - and discovers for himself what Jesus can do. This true-to-life story reveals the plight of street children worldwide and shows that they too can be won to Christ. "The lot of the street children of the world is a guilty secret that needs to be exposed and addressed. This book does it admirably." - Stuart Briscoe

Operation World
21st Century Edition
Patrick Johnstone & Jason Mandryk
ISBN: 1-85078-357-8

The definitive prayer handbook for the church is now available in its 21st Century Edition containing 80% new material! Packed with informative and inspiring fuel for prayer about every country in the world, *Operation World* is essential reading for anyone who wants to make a difference! Over 2,000,000 in print! Recipient of a 2002 ECPA Gold Medallion Book Award.

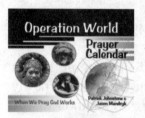

Operation World Prayer Calendar
ISBN: 1-884543-59-6

This spiral desk calendar contains clear graphics and useful geographic, cultural, economic, and political statistics on 122 countries of the world, the *Operation World Prayer Calendar* is a great tool to help you pray intelligently for the world. Pray for each country for three days and see how God works!

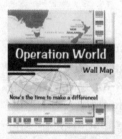

Operation World Wall Map
22" x 36"
ISBN: 1-884543-60-X (Laminated)
ISBN: 1-884543-61-8 (Folded)

This beautiful, full-color wall map is a great way to locate the countries each day that you are praying for and build a global picture. Not only an excellent resource for schools, churches, and offices, but a valuable tool for the home.

The Challenge of Missions
Oswald J. Smith
ISBN: 1-884543-02-2

Almost 2000 years have passed and the desire of Jesus that all should hear his good news is as strong as ever. In this remarkable book Oswald J. Smith maintains that the church which takes this command seriously will experience the blessing of God. *The Challenge of Missions*, which has sold more than 100,000 copies since its first publication, remains compelling reading in this period of exciting growth of the Church worldwide.

Dr. Thomas Hale's Tales of Nepal

Living Stones of the Himalayas
ISBN: 1-884543-35-9
Don't Let the Goats Eat the Loquat Trees
ISBN: 1-884543-36-7
On the Far Side of Liglig Mountain
ISBN: 1-884543-34-0

These fascinating accounts of the true-life stories of doctors Tom and Cynthia Hale share everyday and incredible experiences of life with the beguiling character and personalities of the Nepalese people. In sharing these experiences the reader is truly transported to a most enchanting land.

Also from OM Literature

Challenge of Missions
By Oswald J. Smith

Almost 2000 years have passed and the desire of Jesus that all should hear his good news is as strong as ever. In this remarkable book Oswald J. Smith maintains that the church which takes this command seriously will experience the blessing of God.

> *"Go into all the world and preach the gospel...."* Mark 16:15

ISBN: 18845-4302-2

Also from OM Literature

Priority One: What God Wants
By Norm Lewis

"*Priority One* is a book you should read at all cost. It is about your life. It will change your life."

Dr. Robert Browning
Far East Broadcasting

"*Priority One* speaks truth plainly. Christians who are committed to its goals will help the Church recapture its original role to take the gospel to everyone and make disciples of all nations."

Dr. Bill Bright
Campus Crusade for Christ

ISBN: 08780-8215-8

Also from OM Literature

The Great Omission
A Biblical Basis for World Evangelism
By Robertson McQuilkin

"How come? With so many unreached people, how come
so few Christians are going?" For Robertson McQuilkin
this is one burning question that must be dealt with. He
thoroughly investigates the reasons so few Christians
attempt to carry the message of Christ to "so many" who
have never heard of Him.

ISBN: 18845-4323-5